TRIUMPH
BOOKS

Cleveland Rocked

Cleveland Rocked

The Personalities, Sluggers, and Magic of the 1995 Indians

Zack Meisel

TRIUMPH
B O O K S

No part of this publication may be reproduced, stored in a retrieval system, or transmitted in any form by any means, electronic, mechanical, photocopying, or otherwise, without the prior written permission of the publisher, Triumph Books LLC, 814 North Franklin Street, Chicago, Illinois 60610.

Library of Congress Cataloging-in-Publication Data available upon request.

This book is available in quantity at special discounts for your group or organization. For further information, contact:

Triumph Books LLC
814 North Franklin Street
Chicago, Illinois 60610
(312) 337-0747
www.triumphbooks.com

Printed in U.S.A.
ISBN: 978-1-62937-773-5

Design by Patricia Frey
Photos courtesy of AP Images unless otherwise indicated

To my great-uncle Mike, one of many who deserves to witness just one World Series triumph for his longtime devotion to Cleveland's baseball team. And to a courageous friend and colleague, Matt Loede, who has always set the greatest example by cherishing every moment he spends at the ballpark.

Contents

Foreword

UNTIL MY DAD RETIRED IN 1978, my brother and I would go to batting practice and shag fly balls and hang around the ballpark with Major League Baseball players. I have memories of my dad playing winter ball in Ponce and Santurce in Puerto Rico, where I had the opportunity to interact with the players.

Roberto and I definitely wanted to be like our dad. We were so familiar with baseball. It was everything we knew.

When we played Little League, we had an advantage from learning things in a professional way. Not to say we had better instincts, but we knew how to play the game at an earlier age than the other kids. We had ideas of where to be and how to do things.

When we finished the school year, we would travel to the U.S. to see our dad play in the big leagues. When he retired, we played baseball year-round. We were more entertained that way.

I signed with the Padres first, and when I got to minor league spring training and I saw all of the competition, it's not that I had doubts, but it was just like, *Wow, I have to compete against all of these people who are good.* There were some good catchers. But I knew that I was young and I had time to develop. When you sign a professional baseball contract, you basically play for 30 teams, especially when you're in the minor leagues. You don't know if you're going to be with that organization in the big leagues.

When I went to Triple-A and started performing well, I knew my path was blocked by Benito Santiago. I ran out of options. I knew one of us was going to be traded, whether it was Benito or myself, and I figured since I was the younger, more affordable guy, it would be easier for any organization to deal with the lower salary. So I was expecting to be traded.

I had an opportunity to get a September call-up in 1988 and '89. I had a chance to play with my brother. And then I got traded to Cleveland.

The funny thing is, when I got traded to Cleveland, we had won two minor league championships with the Padres. So Carlos Baerga, who was traded with me, and I had an idea of what winning was all about, just not at this level. All my experience in 1991, '92, and '93 was nothing but development and failure and not knowing how to close games. I was more than five years removed from winning in the minor leagues before I had a chance to enjoy a celebration of clinching a division. When we did that in '95, it erased a lot of bad memories from the early '90s.

And that season, I almost did not play a single game. I had microfracture surgery, and at the time, there was no precedent for that kind of operation. They told me I was going to miss the year, but I was able to come back at the end of June.

There was a special magic at the stadium that year. And the fans— it was so loud every night. They expected us to come back. We had the offense that created traffic and had power on top of that. It was remarkable, one through nine. The offensive numbers and records they put up, it was ridiculous. It was infectious, the way the guys were hitting.

I believe that was our most complete team. When you're talking about versatility and a balanced offense, you had guys who could hit for power, who could hit for average, who had speed. We have never had a lineup like that since.

I had help from Tony Peña with catching. He was very good to me. There was talent in Carlos Baerga, Kenny Lofton, Jim Thome, Manny Ramirez, and Albert Belle and we were supported by Eddie Murray, who came from a great pedigree and knew how to win. It was a good recipe for us young guys. We had to turn that corner and turn that talent into superstardom, and that's what we did.

I remember when we lost the World Series, half of the locker room was crying. Whenever we lose, I don't like to see the other team celebrate. I walk inside right away. At that time, I knew that the journey wasn't complete, and that's one of the reasons I'm still around here. But I was pleased that we did a fantastic job representing Cleveland and the Indians franchise.

I was five years old when I started going to the ballpark with my dad. I have seen a lot of baseball. I played plenty and I enjoy what I'm doing now, mentoring young guys and coaching. It has been fun for me, especially with this organization. After I left Cleveland, I didn't see one postseason. All the postseason experience, all the winning experiences I had were in Cleveland.

I tell everybody, all those accolades and all those clutch hits, they are highlights from my career, especially the ones from the postseason. But the moment that I really cherish the most is when we raised that banner in '95 after so many years of losing. That meant a lot to me. It erased all those losing years and brought a new era to Cleveland, and I felt very proud to be part of the beginning of the new generation of the Cleveland Indians.

—Sandy Alomar Jr.

Foreword

WHERE DOES TIME GO?

In '94, the strike hit. We were good. I don't know where we would have ended up in '94, but we knew we had something special. I think the strike kept our team very hungry, focused, and ready to go in '95, and we showed it with the way we played.

Offensively, we had a tremendous lineup from top to bottom. We had speed. We had power. We had youth. We had veteran pitching.

And then when we got to the World Series, it was like, "Yeah, this is what it's all about." We all dreamed of it, but we didn't really know the process. We didn't know what it was like to be in a World Series. The first night in Atlanta, I remember being introduced on the baseline as a 25-year-old kid and I went, *Oh, my gosh, this is what you dream of.*

In your backyard, you envision being in a moment like that. We all were gifted and granted that opportunity to do it. It was an emotion that's hard to explain. And then only going one other time, in '97, now looking back—I never took that for granted. I really didn't. It just goes to show you how special those moments are. In everybody's career, there are moments that stand out. To me, at an early age, that was one of the biggest highlights, if not the biggest, just because we dream of a World Series. You pinch yourself.

I felt confident, but I don't know if I felt like I did later in my career. You were always trying to get better. Early on, I had struggles. I had defensive struggles. At times, I wouldn't play against left-handed pitching. But that year—I don't want to call it a breakout year, but it was a year that I felt like, finally, I could be put in a moment that was like that in the World Series.

And there come struggles. Obviously, when you face a pitching staff like the Braves, there are those moments. You can't be a hero in every at-bat. That's what I learned very quickly. They had great pitching. But when you do have that special moment, you bottle that up and you want to keep that moment. You don't want it to ever leave.

Carlos Baerga was the ringleader, the way he was as a person, as a teammate. And then you add Omar Vizquel, you add Kenny Lofton, you add Albert Belle. Even our bench guys. We were just a close-knit, special group of guys who truly, at the end of the day, cared about each other and really wanted to be there for each other and do well with each other. Guys like Albert and Kenny, the really great, really talented players we had, pushed each other to get better. You wanted to be good.

That was the year we started putting bubble gum on everybody's hats. There were just fun things we did that made our team exciting to watch, along with the fact that we had tremendous players who were all young and coming on or were established and had been there. When you bring in Eddie Murray and Orel Hershiser and Dennis Martínez, these guys had great résumés. It was fun.

And then you get done with the season and, yes, guys would go to Florida or back to their hometown, but they still wanted to come back, even in the winter, to work out and to be a part of what we had, which was special. We didn't want to be away from each other for too long. That's how close we were. Guys like Baerga, Vizquel, and Lofton, they were a big part of that. They made it fun to be their teammate.

Still, to this day, I have friends who will go, "Man, to come to Cleveland in the '90s, especially in '95, was just so much fun." The number of come-from-behind wins. It was great to be a part of it.

The '95 season was so special because it was the beginning. It started the first part of the sellout streak. It was great to be a Cleveland Indian. It was an exciting time in Cleveland. It put us on the map to where we, after that year, expected to go back. That's when John Hart and Dan O'Dowd and Mark Shapiro were constructing our team to put us in a position to make a long term run, and we did that. We did it for many years in the '90s.

It set the bar high very quickly after the strike in '94. And then '95 was just magical. For me, getting to be an established player, I couldn't have asked to be on a better ball club and learn the ropes at an early age.

—Jim Thome

Introduction

THERE'S NO BETTER EVIDENCE than the sea of fans wearing Cleveland Indians garb and standing in place for hours on a chilly Monday afternoon at the end of October...after the Indians had *lost* the 1995 World Series. That season meant so much to so many people. Even with the undesired final result, that team still accomplished much more than any of the 40 iterations that came before it. The group captivated a city. It reintroduced to the masses what competent baseball looked like. It made believers out of the nearly 3 million people who passed through the turnstiles at Jacobs Field. It launched an era of Indians baseball that created a generation of baseball fans.

For the athletes, sports are about pushing limits and harnessing competitive spirit. Games and seasons are characterized by glory and agony. For the fans, it's about the mental Rolodex. Each game is a new opportunity to file away another memory, triumphant or traumatic. For the grandest sports events in our lives, we can remember the location of the TV, our companions on the couch, or the recipient of the first post-buzzer high-five at the bar. We can place ourselves on that barstool or on that leather sofa, at the 35-yard line, or a few rows behind third base.

We change jobs, expand our families, and move around the globe, but those moments are frozen in time. We can remember the emotion we felt in the immediate aftermath of victory or defeat. It's much fuzzier how we felt in the minutes and seconds leading up to that defining moment.

The 1995 Indians served as my introduction to sports. (I know, I know—if only we all could be so fortunate.) I can remember the dimly lit living room where I watched the Indians and Braves square off in Game 6 of the World Series in late October. I was at my grandmother's friend's house, of all places. It was fitting that I watched with her as Albert Belle and Kenny Lofton battled Tom Glavine and David Justice. My grandmother never demonstrated much of a devotion to sports until I pursued a career as a sportswriter. Then she would boast about how Jim Brown used to gawk at her when she and her friends watched Browns practices from behind a chain-link fence at a local high school. She supplied story ideas that probably only interested her, prompts about baseball card collections and rookie hazing rituals and Gaylord Perry's whereabouts.

When Tom Hamilton joined the Indians' broadcast team for the 1990 season, he figured the sad-sack Indians would be a competitive team. "I thought in spring training, 'Damn. We're going to win the pennant,'" he once told me. His partner on the mic, Herb Score, told him not to kid himself, but also instructed him not to let the team's deficiencies influence his work ethic or effort behind his craft. That '90 club went 77–85 before plummeting to 105 losses the following season. It would be another few years before Hamilton had much to shriek about on the radio. The players' strike halted the Indians' momentum in '94, but in '95, for the first time in 41 years, the team provided the sort of season that everyone could wrap their arms around and embrace, the sort of summer Hamilton and so many others had long envisioned.

For four decades, fans clamored to attend Opening Day at Municipal Stadium and maybe another game or two once Lake Erie thawed. As long as a certain magazine avoided some foolishly bold proclamations, few held lofty expectations for the Indians. And then a new ballpark bloomed from previously neglected soil in downtown Cleveland. A talented roster soon followed. And by 1995, fans had reason to believe, something so simple, yet something that had proven elusive for a long time.

The '95 Indians were responsible for a litany of those moments that linger for years and decades, be it one of the regular season walk-off home runs, Tony Peña's 2:00 AM heroics, Belle's biceps flex, or Lofton's 180-foot scamper in Seattle. It was the blossoming of a tight-knit bond between a collection of characters in the clubhouse and the swarms of fans who gravitated toward them. And it kept everyone on the edge of their seats, be it at the ballpark, the local watering hole, or on the living room couch.

1

This Is How We Do It

CARLOS BAERGA CAN STILL KEEP the tune, years later, in his booming baritone.

This is how we do it.

"That was one of the songs that started it," Kenny Lofton says, "and once it started, it didn't stop."

Each hand in the clubhouse clutched a dark green bottle of champagne, the foamy substance spilling down the side of the glass. Each player tossed a white CENTRAL DIVISION CHAMPIONS T-shirt over his uniform. Owner Dick Jacobs, in his cream-colored button-down shirt and tie, received the first champagne shower, with Baerga and Tony Peña playing the role of ringleaders. Jacobs was able to remove his blazer and his glasses, but the rest of his dressy ensemble was drenched. He wiped the bubbly from his face and laughed it off. It's not like this had become a regular occasion...yet.

The players made general manager John Hart a popular target. He placed a CENTRAL DIVISION CHAMPIONS hat atop his head and made the rounds, hugging players and thanking them for their performances. They returned the favor by pouring beer down his back, a chilly surprise that would make any unsuspecting victim jump. Players interrupted a Mike Hargrove TV interview by dumping a gray bucket of brew on their manager. Hargrove participated in the mischief, too.

As Julian Tavarez wandered around the clubhouse filled with soaking teammates, coaches, and media members, he shouted that familiar refrain.

This is how we do it.

He and Manny Ramirez jumped up and down as they hugged and howled the lyrics—painfully off-key, yet never having sounded so perfect.

This is how we do it. It's Friday night. And I feel all right.

Some players stood on the periphery, nursing a beer near their locker as they surveyed the pandemonium unfolding in the center of the clubhouse. And then there were those in the middle of the madness, their T-shirts soaked enough to reveal the red lettering of the name and number on their jersey.

Montell Jordan released his hit song—his first single—in February 1995. "This Is How We Do It" spent seven weeks atop the Billboard Hot 100 and R&B singles charts. And it became the theme song of the 1995 Indians, a team that proved all summer it did things its own way.

"This is how we do it," Baerga said, reminiscing about the team's mentality nearly a quarter-century later. "We come to play every day. We play hard every day. No matter who we play, we're gonna kill you."

Yeah, that sounds harsh. But that is the approach that group maintained. They arrived at Jacobs Field each afternoon on a mission.

"'Who's pitching for them?'" said Lofton, a friend and fraternity brother of Jordan. "'Let's go kick their butt.' That's the idea and the mindset we had. 'Who was on the mound? What was their ERA?' We didn't give a damn. Bring it."

And then after the game, if the Indians emerged victorious—and the vast majority of the time, they did—someone pressed play on that familiar tune and the celebration commenced.

"No matter what," Lofton said. "We could win by 10 runs. We could win by a walk-off. The music's still going. Everybody's going crazy in the clubhouse, like it was a walk-off every game."

This was not a collection of best friends who all sacrificed for the betterment of the team. There were disputes and confrontations, broken bats and broken thermostats. There were personality clashes and supersized egos. But there was a clubhouse stocked with talent, a dugout full of driven players fixated on a common goal: destroying the opponent.

"You know what? I can't call it chemistry," Lofton said. "I would call it chaos. But it worked. See, and that's the thing—maybe you could say chemistry can work with chaos if it's total chaos. It's hard to explain it. I'll say it this way: chaos worked for us. It doesn't work for everyone. But I think because of the team we had and the players we had, chaos worked. We just wanted to have so much fun that it turned into fun chaos."

Fun chaos.

Is that a common manner of assessing a team?

"Never," Lofton said. "You don't get that kind of team."

One victory stood between that chaos-fueled team and those bottles of booze on that cool Friday night in September 1995.

Jim Thome could not recall the batter. The second the baseball ascended toward Orion's belt, Thome cared about nothing else but corralling it with his glove. The batter's identity did not matter. The opponent did not matter. The score did not matter.

Catch the ball. Squeeze it tight. Find your teammates. Celebrate a long-awaited playoff berth.

So, no—Thome, nearly a quarter-century later, could not remember the name of the fellow in the gray uniform who skied the pop-up in his vicinity. That was the question posed to him, though, during an All-Star Game symposium in downtown Cleveland on a sunny July morning in 2019. Which Baltimore Orioles hitter made the final out that landed the Indians the American League Central Division title?

Cal Ripken Jr. had grounded out to start the ninth inning against Tribe closer Jose Mesa. Fellow Hall of Famer Harold Baines followed with a fly out. Catcher Chris Hoiles, the tying run, walked and was replaced at first base by Jeffrey Hammonds. It was not Brady Anderson, Rafael Palmeiro, or Bobby Bonilla, three familiar sluggers who had all batted the previous inning.

No, the answer to the trivia question—which stumped Thome— was Jeff Huson, a veteran utility infielder who hardly wielded a threatening piece of lumber. Huson popped out to Thome, who clenched the division-clinching out in his glove, kept his left arm raised high above his head, and scampered to the center of the diamond to join his teammates in a dog pile.

There was no uncertainty, no surprise, no last-minute overcoming of obstacles to seize control of the American League Central. This had been telegraphed for months. The Indians boasted an 85–37 record on the morning of September 8. They possessed an insurmountable 22½-game lead on their division foes. The 41,656 fans who filed into Jacobs Field on that Friday night all knew what would likely unfold following the top of the ninth.

But that did not make the moment any less sweet. When Thome secured the final out, the Indians guaranteed their first foray into October in 41 years. Broadcaster Tom Hamilton shouted, "The season of dreams has become a reality! Cleveland, you will have an October to remember."

The Indians coaches embraced in the home dugout as fireworks exploded in the sky high above the outfield. The players exchanged bear hugs and handshakes on the infield grass. They emptied the contents of a Gatorade cooler onto their manager, who shed a tear during the celebration. They later shifted the festivities to, appropriately, a TGI Fridays restaurant in nearby Westlake, where many of the players and coaches resided during the season.

The franchise was so synonymous with losing, Hollywood unveiled a blockbuster hit in the late '80s to parody the embarrassment that the decades of ineptitude had fostered. Hargrove guided the club out of that pit of misery and into the postseason. One fan in attendance raised a sign that simply read: FINALLY.

Another sign read: DEAL WITH IT, AMERICA...CLEVELAND INDIANS...BEST TEAM IN BASEBALL. That sort of message would have triggered laughter if presented at Municipal Stadium during the old venue's final 35 years or so of hosting the Indians' home games. The team that had become so familiar with the AL East basement, the team that piled up 101 losses after *Sports Illustrated* placed Joe Carter and Cory Snyder on its season-preview cover and declared the Indians the class of the AL, the team that had not amassed more than 87 wins in a season since the Eisenhower administration—that team stood tall above its peers in the standings. Upon clinching the playoff spot, the front office received congratulatory phone calls from former players, including Duane Kuiper, Gary Bell, Max Alvis, and Pat Tabler. Former Cleveland Browns head coach Sam Rutigliano penned a note commending the team on capturing the attention of the city.

After the game, as the fireworks persisted above the left-field scoreboard, the team raised a flag in center field to signify its accomplishment. Lofton pulled the lever as Garth Brooks' "The Dance" blared on the ballpark sound system, per Hargrove's request. Brooks' ballad was the favorite song of former Tribe reliever Steve Olin. During spring training in 1993, Olin and bullpen mate Tim Crews died in a boating accident on Little Lake Nellie in Clermont, Florida, a harrowing tragedy that rocked the franchise for a long time. Tears streamed down the players' faces as they paid tribute on that momentous evening two and a half years later.

The Indians' emergence did not happen overnight. The 1995 season was marked by majestic home runs, walk-off wins, and "This Is How We Do It" serving as the soundtrack for an almost nightly clubhouse bash. But the franchise endured plenty of pain along its path to that season, and though those in the front office maintained high hopes for the club, no one truly knew what to expect.

Hargrove addressed the team during spring training. He provided a history lesson on the Indians, waxing poetic about the late '40s and early '50s, about the 1920 and 1948 championship teams, and about the Hall of Fame talent that had passed through Cleveland—icons such as Lou Boudreau and Bob Feller and Al Rosen and Larry Doby. He also revisited the franchise's four decades of misery following those golden years—not that the players needed a reminder.

The Indians' postseason drought had reached its 41st year. This was not the first time in that span that a Cleveland club had arrived at spring training with lofty expectations. The others fizzled, often emphatically. There is no better example than that '87 team, with Carter and Snyder posing as *Sports Illustrated* cover models. That club, projected by the magazine's day-job-keeping soothsayers to win the World Series, started the season 1–10, en route to a 61–101 record. Swing and an epic miss. Hargrove explained to the group that it had the potential to be special, to wind up on the preferred side of history, to leave a mark as the team that reversed the franchise's fortunes.

"Probably in '93, the end of '93 going into '94, you could feel it," Hargrove said. "In '92 and '93, our record was identical. We had an identical win/loss record at the end of both of those seasons, but the difference in the '92 and '93 seasons, in '93, we were able to carry it on through the '94 season. Guys really believed in themselves. I think getting Eddie Murray really helped a lot. Dennis Martínez really helped a lot, as far as knowing how to win.

"You learn to win just like you learn to walk. And our guys had enough big-league experience by that time. They had the belief that they could play with anybody."

And they did precisely that. One hundred wins, despite a strike-shortened, 144-game schedule. League-best totals in nearly every hitting and pitching category. A massive advantage in the standings—not just on their division rivals, but on just about every team in the sport. No other team in the league won more than 90 games.

"The season was just a magical season," Hargrove said. "It was like the perfect storm. We just beat people to death with our bats. We scored a lot of runs. The thing that struck me with that team, that made it so magical, other than the 27 come-from-behind victories, was the fact that there never was a bump in the road with that ball club all year long. There was not one dramatic incident that could have derailed what we were trying to do.

"I had never had it before, and I have never had it since."

The Indians captivated the city and invited Indians fans on an unforgettable ride that persisted until the end of October, a time in the calendar that had never before been reserved for baseball in Cleveland, for extra-inning walk-off hits through air brisk enough to reveal one's breath, for controversially flexible strike zones, for police escorts and downtown parades and heartfelt speeches.

The story of the '95 Indians really starts about seven years earlier, though. So, let's rewind to the beginning, when the organization planted the seeds that eventually sprouted into perhaps the most memorable season in franchise history.

This is, in fact, how the Indians did it.

2

"Even the Toilet Looked Better"

MARK SHAPIRO SCALED A NARROW, crooked staircase to reach the executive offices for his job interview. When he entered John Hart's office, he spotted missing ceiling tiles, a plastic plant, and a space heater near the general manager's desk.

As he sat down, ready to deliver his sales pitch on why he deserved an opportunity to join the organization's brain trust, he thought to himself: *This is a major league general manager's office? You have to be kidding me. This is unbelievable.*

No, this was just old Cleveland Stadium.

Everyone kept a space heater at his or her desk, because the heat in the building rarely functioned.

"It just seemed like it was always wet and cold," said Tom Hamilton, the Indians' radio broadcast voice since 1990. "It didn't seem like it warmed up until July."

Hamilton remembers the lopsided losses in early April, when his attention would drift toward the chunks of ice bobbing on the choppy waters of Lake Erie in the distance. Aside from Opening Day, the home finale, and perhaps a holiday or two, Cleveland Stadium remained mostly abandoned during baseball season. From his perch in the radio booth, Hamilton could hear every word muttered in the venue. During one game, in which Tribe shortstop Felix Fermin was faring well at the plate, Tigers pitcher Frank Tanana said to his catcher, "Ah, just tell him what's coming. We can't do any worse."

When Sandy Alomar Jr. crouched behind home plate, he could hear fans shouting from the outfield bleachers—plus the echo that carried every word. Jim Thome had to learn to tune out the hecklers who badgered him after every errant throw from third base. His dad, Chuck, would remind him that Ted Williams, Babe Ruth, and Bob Feller all played on the same field.

"You could hear people yell from one side of the ballpark to the other, because it was like a gigantic mausoleum and no one was ever there," said Dan O'Dowd, the club's director of player development and, beginning in 1993, assistant general manager.

In the fall, once the Browns began their season, yard markers would remain in the grass during baseball games. When he played in the '70s and early '80s, Rick Manning would occasionally call for a fair catch before hauling in a fly ball in center field.

"You always knew you were not the main attraction there," Hamilton said.

When O'Dowd arrived at his office each morning, he flickered the lights and jumped up and down so startled mice would scurry away.

"They looked well-fed," Hamilton said. "They were chubby mice. They never had a lack of food."

In fact, the rodents enjoyed a better spread than the ones the players received. There was no kitchen, just a refrigerator stocked with peanut butter and jelly sandwiches and tin cans of tuna fish. The postgame spread typically included those delicacies, cheese and crackers, slices of pepperoni, or whatever leftovers team officials could scrounge up from the concession stands. The freezer contained Dixie cups of ice for pitchers' arms and ice cream bars intended for sweet-toothed closer Doug Jones. The dugouts were small. The bathrooms were grimy.

Simply put, the building offered no amenities, no competitive advantages to aid a bumbling franchise.

"It was terrible," Shapiro said. "I think some of the people who were from Cleveland felt some nostalgia for it, but it was a terrible work environment. It was a terrible place for the players to train."

The cramped clubhouse regularly ran out of space, so September call-ups and players who landed on the injured list had to haul their belongings upstairs to an auxiliary locker room. In the back of the training room, near the refrigerator, sat a curl bar and a couple of dumbbells. That served as the weight room. In the offseason, when the Browns seized control of the building, the Indians used a cage in the laundry room in the basement at Lutheran Hospital as their weight room.

The batting cage—yes, that is singular—resided underneath the outfield bleachers, an inconvenient hike from the clubhouse and an upstream trek through a sea of fans on the concourse once the ballpark gates opened to the public. For the 1991 season, the Indians pushed back the outfield fences. And then the team scored the fewest runs in baseball en route to a league-high 105 losses, the highest total in franchise history.

Catcher Sandy Alomar Jr. referred to the venue as a graveyard, pointing to the wind blowing in from Lake Erie as the primary culprit. The Indians mustered only 22 home runs in 82 home games. In all, the Indians totaled 79 home runs, 36 fewer than the second-lowest total by an American League team.

Center fielder Kenny Lofton: "The whole stadium was a bad stadium, to be honest. But it's what Cleveland had."

Alomar: "You had the desire to go to the ballpark. You get there early to work and it can help you in the long run. But the old stadium, it's like, you get there and it was kind of demoralizing. Everyone made fun of it."

Shapiro: "That stadium was a terrible place to play baseball. It was a terrible place to watch baseball. There was very little redeeming about it."

Starting pitcher Charles Nagy selected three words to describe the structure: big, gray, and dreary.

"There was nothing to look forward to," he said. "You showed up and you played baseball and you went home."

It didn't help matters that the Indians were closing in on their fourth consecutive decade without postseason action.

But then the referendum passed.

Commissioner Fay Vincent sat in a golf cart behind home plate during Indians batting practice one afternoon when a swarm of reporters surrounded him. Vincent did not skirt the issue. If a measure for a new stadium did not pass on the May 1990 ballot, he could not guarantee that the major league team would remain in Cleveland long term.

Bob DiBiasio, the public relations director at the time, had two phone lines installed in his house, tied directly to the newsrooms at the *Tampa Tribune* and the *Denver Post*. Both cities sought a professional baseball team, and both planned to pounce if the referendum failed. Issue 2 sparked plenty of debate. Some wanted the money assigned to some other project. Mayor Michael White argued that a new ballpark would revitalize a neglected area of downtown Cleveland and that it made good business sense for the community.

"That's why you could talk about Dick Jacobs' ownership being one of the most significant ownerships of our franchise," DiBiasio said, "because of the timing and his ability—building buildings downtown and having the ability to walk into the mayor's office and say, 'You're building me a new ballpark. We're going to get this done.'"

A motion to build a football and baseball dome a few years earlier died a quick and painless death. The new arrangement, which eventually became Gateway Plaza, included a basketball arena next door to the baseball stadium. And it felt like a last-gasp effort to keep the baseball team in town. Jacobs no longer wanted to be a tenant on the shores of Lake Erie. It was not in his DNA. Jacobs was a developer, so he had a team of architects and engineers handy to fuel the planning process.

DiBiasio composed a pair of press releases, one for if the issue passed, with a colorful, uplifting, enthusiastic quote from ownership. And the other?

"You do your dance on the other one for the quote from ownership," he said.

The Indians hoped that one would never see the light of day. O'Dowd and his wife monitored the election results from their home in Avon Lake.

"It was scary," he said. "Leading up to the vote, there were so many polls being taken that said it wouldn't pass. Early in the evening, it was being defeated. And then it passed by a very small margin at the end."

Issue 2 passed by about 13,000 votes, 51.7 percent to 48.3 percent.

"It snuck through and then became probably the most significant moment in franchise history," DiBiasio said, "or there's a good chance we wouldn't be playing baseball."

DiBiasio sent the more pleasant press release to the Associated Press, *The Plain Dealer*, and the *Akron Beacon Journal* before he relayed the news to the *Tampa Tribune* and the *Denver Post*. He dialed the phone number, placed the phone in the coupler, and the cylinder rotated to transmit the message. DiBiasio estimated it took about 12 minutes to send one page.

Timing was everything. The Indians' brain trust aimed to turn loose a talented roster right as the group shifted into the new ballpark.

"It played out even more perfect than the vision," O'Dowd said.

Team president Hank Peters convinced owners Dick and David Jacobs to buy into a long term blueprint. The Indians front office would restock the farm system, acquiring young, controllable assets via trades and then, when the time was right—preferably in conjunction with the opening of the new facility—the club would fill in the remaining gaps with seasoned veteran players. The first domino to fall (in December 1989) was the trade of slugger Joe Carter for Alomar and Baerga, a pair of prospects with the San Diego Padres.

Remember that painful 1991 season, the six-month pit of despair that produced more than a hundred losses and more than a thousand groans, the sort of season that resembles a funeral procession and forces fans to wonder if the investment of following along is worth their time and energy? O'Dowd actually singles out that year as the turning point, the first bit of evidence that the franchise was headed on the proper path.

In his first tour of regular big-league playing time, Albert Belle delivered a .282 batting average and a .540 slugging percentage, with 28 home runs, 31 doubles, and a manageable number of headaches. Carlos Baerga, in his first full season, blossomed as the club's No. 3 hitter.

During the season, Mike Hargrove replaced John McNamara as manager and John Hart was promoted to general manager. The

Indians selected Manny Ramirez, Herbert Perry, and Chad Ogea—three contributing members of the '95 team—with their first three picks in the amateur draft that summer. Jim Thome made his major league debut that September. Nagy recorded his first full season in the big leagues, logging 211 innings to set up an All-Star campaign the following year. After the season, the team converted catcher Eddie Taubensee into Lofton in a lopsided trade with the Houston Astros and acquired Paul Sorrento in a deal with the Minnesota Twins.

"We didn't have any young talent when we started," said O'Dowd, who oversaw the club's farm system.

That would quickly change, but not without clearing some hurdles first. When pressure mounted from the front office to sever ties with Belle, a surly slugger with unpredictable antics, O'Dowd pleaded with Peters to change his mind, since the organization faced a shortage of skilled prospects. But after some shrewd trades, some better drafting, and an added emphasis on prospect development, the Indians started to pile up talent. And with the knowledge that they would soon escape the hungry rodents and the plummeting ceiling tiles, there was a fresh source of energy in the front office.

"We really, really thought we were on to something," O'Dowd said. "We were doing analytics before analytics were being done. We were studying things differently than anybody in the game. Our multi-year contracts were a strategy that caught the industry completely by surprise. I don't know what Apple or Google or any of these startup high-tech companies are like, but I would think we had a very similar environment going on there. The energy level, the level of intellect we had in the office, we had so many smart, young guys—every single day was a really cool adventure. In my 35 years of being involved in running or helping to run clubs, that was the best time for me in the game."

Meanwhile, the vision for the ballpark was starting to come together. Jim Folk joined the organization on June 1, 1992, to oversee the construction of the venue. In his role as director of ballpark operations, he would work with the design team and the construction team to get the place built, get it open, and keep it running. At the time, new ballparks were popping up across the country. Folk had a hand in the processes in Chicago and St. Petersburg, where, respectively, new Comiskey Park (now Guaranteed Rate Field) and the Florida Suncoast Dome (now Tropicana Field) were erected a few years before Jacobs Field sprouted up from the downtown Cleveland dirt. Toronto had opened the SkyDome in 1989. Baltimore opened Oriole Park at Camden Yards in 1992. The Colorado Rockies were preparing to open Coors Field, and the Texas Rangers were readying the Ballpark at Arlington.

"The floodgates were open," Folk said. "Baltimore really tipped the scales. Baltimore really busted the thinking on these things."

Camden Yards was the new standard to follow. New Comiskey was what Folk deemed "the last of the old breed," a "big fortress" that had to sit at street level because of drainage issues, as opposed to most of the new parks, which sat below street level, so fans would walk in on the main concourse and head down steps to their seats. Folk likened the dome in St. Petersburg to Kauffman Stadium in Kansas City, just with a roof on it...and without a baseball team to occupy it. The Rays did not exist until 1998, so for nearly a decade, that ballpark hosted concerts, tractor pulls, and home and garden shows. It also landed the largest crowd, at the time, for a basketball game in the state of Florida, as 25,710 fans watched the Chicago Bulls play an exhibition game against the Seattle Supersonics in 1990. (A New

Kids on the Block concert attracted nearly twice as many fans about two months earlier.)

Camden Yards changed everything.

"Baltimore just opened the floodgates for all of these neat, retro ballparks with all of the modern amenities," Folk said, "so you have suites and club seats and you have a concourse that more than two people can walk on at the same time. You have enough bathrooms and good sight lines in the seating bowl. Baltimore was the test case and they really did a great job with it."

Shapiro joined the Indians' front office before the 1992 season, right as the structures between Ontario Street and E. 9th Street met their demise. Shapiro lived at Reserve Square at the time, a few blocks from where the Gateway Plaza would eventually surface. One of his first weekends living in downtown Cleveland, they imploded a cold storage warehouse, the final building standing in the way of the construction site for the new ballpark.

"Literally, my whole building shook," Shapiro said. "I was scared to death. I didn't know what was going on."

Hamilton can recall driving past the surface parking lot, the eventual site for the stadium, and shrugging his shoulders.

"You were just like, 'Huh?' I couldn't fathom," he said. "How are you going to get a ballpark on this plot of land? It was just inconceivable."

When Folk arrived in Cleveland, the Indians had initiated the excavation process. They had a massive hole in the ground. They just needed to fill it with a structure that could host 40,000-some people, 50 baseball players, a couple of coaching staffs, and four umpires. Folk oversaw the first concrete pour in the dugout suites and the dugouts, and the placement of the first piece of steel.

On June 25, 1992, the Indians installed home plate in the proper position before a gathering of suite holders, players, employees, and media members. DiBiasio convinced all three local TV stations to start their 6:00 PM broadcasts with a live shot of the ceremony. Nagy and Mel Harder, who delivered the first pitch at the old stadium 60 years earlier, completed ceremonial tosses to Alomar. Harder wore his off-white uniform with a giant Block C on the left side of his chest. He sported high socks and a pair of black Nike shoes. Nagy donned his typical home get-up, a white uniform with a red and navy stripe down each shoulder and pant leg.

As everyone else in attendance dined and celebrated the occasion, Nagy and Harder chatted down the left-field line. The 82-year-old taught the 25-year-old where to position his fingers on the seams for a particular breaking ball. The Indians' photographer captured the moment.

After that meeting, Harder would occasionally call DiBiasio with a request during Indians games.

Bobby, you need to have Charlie call me. He's sneaking over the rubber a bit. He's cutting to the plate. He's limiting his strike zone.

DiBiasio would relay the recommendations to Nagy or to pitching coach Mark Wiley, which would make Harder's day.

"Mel was always very near and dear to my heart," Nagy said. "He always took the time. We always liked to sit down and just talk baseball and talk pitching. A great man. I was very fortunate to have met him and built a friendship with him. That day was special."

Home plate was the centerpiece. It had to face north-to-northeast to shield the sun from the hitters' eyes. Once they placed it, they could sketch out the rest of the puzzle. They could pencil in the pitcher's mound, the bases, center field, and the foul lines and designate the distances to the retaining wall behind the plate and from the field to the main concourse.

Once every four to six weeks, players and front office members would ride a bus to the construction site to view the progress. They wore hard hats and listened to a tour guide prattle on about the state-of-the-art 17,000-square foot batting cages, the SwimEX pool, the training room that featured twice as many tables, the sauna and steam room, the video room, and the strength and conditioning area. The planning committee consulted players, coaches, and members of the organization for input on the design of the clubhouse, the field layout, concessions, merchandise areas, even details as minute as the location of a certain door or walkway so people could move from Point A to Point B without creating logistical obstacles.

"We would make trips over there just because of the hope of what that represented to us," O'Dowd said. "It sustained us through some really tough times."

Early on, it was difficult to visualize. When you are conditioned to black-and-white, it can be challenging to imagine vivid colors.

One day, Lofton placed a hard hat atop his head and trotted out to where he was told center field would sit.

"I'm like, 'There's no damn center field. What is this?'" he said. "They were like, 'You're standing in center field.'"

He looked around and tried to envision lush, green grass and sections full of fans in Tribe gear.

"I'm like, 'Wow.' Then, they started to put the stands in and it started to make sense," he said. "'Okay, now I can see what you're talking about.' But at first, I was like, 'Dude, this is just dirt.'"

Sorrento remembers learning about the dimensions of the new building and the studies completed about the Lake Erie wind patterns and their influence on fly balls. He marveled at the design, which placed the field below city level.

Alomar, on the other hand, was discouraged by the 19-foot wall assigned to left field. As a right-handed hitter who regularly yanked pitches to left field, he preferred a shorter fence.

"Why do lefties get the benefit?" he said. "It would have been better if the big scoreboard would have been in right field and they left left field open. I didn't have superstar numbers, but I would have been better. The year Albert hit 50 [home runs], he probably would have hit 60."

The Indians attracted nearly 217,000 fans to Cleveland Stadium for the team's final series at Municipal Stadium. They sold commemorative tickets for the three-game weekend set against the Chicago White Sox. The tickets for the Saturday game included a photo of Harder and Nagy talking shop at the groundbreaking ceremony from about 15 months earlier.

The Browns hosted the Miami Dolphins at the stadium the following week, so the Indians had to protect the building at the conclusion of the series. They anticipated fans might attempt to steal seats or sinks or other infrastructure to stow away as souvenirs. Immediately after the Sunday matinee, the Browns would convert the diamond into a football field, tearing out the infield dirt and knocking down the pitcher's mound. They placed backhoes outside the stadium that afternoon, just waiting for the final pitch so they could pounce. The grounds crew sported tuxedos as they dug up home plate.

The Indians invited Bob Hope—the longtime comedian, actor, singer, dancer, and former minority owner of the franchise—to perform a special rendition of his "Thanks For The Memory" tune prior to the final game at the stadium. Ninety years old at the time, Hope flew in from Paris on a private jet. He requested a masseuse upon arrival in Cleveland at 10:30 PM, the night before the finale.

Hope walked out onto the field—during the middle of White Sox batting practice, mind you—to rehearse. The batting practice pitcher paused the action and the Chicago players greeted Hope and shook his hand. DiBiasio was tasked with escorting Hope around the ballpark. He asked Hope if he wanted a podium to hold his script, to ease the page-turning process. Hope scoffed, insulted at the offer, and reminded DiBiasio he had performed Vaudeville for nearly 75 years without the need for such assistance.

Naturally, when Hope performed his song, he clutched the microphone with his left hand and his script in his right. So every time he flipped the page, he moved the microphone away from his mouth and no one could hear what he was singing.

DiBiasio turned to Hope's wife, Dolores, and said, "We have a little problem here."

"Young man," she replied, "you're on your own."

"It wasn't perfect," DiBiasio recalled, "but I think people got the sentiment. It still made for a remarkable closing of that building to baseball."

A fitting one, for sure.

A week before Jacobs Field opened its doors to the public in 1994, the Indians held a dress rehearsal. They invited the contractors and their families to test every function of the facility. They checked the turnstiles. They used the fryers and the grills. They tested the public address system. They entered all the bathrooms and participated in the Jim Folk Memorial Gang Flush, the ultimate challenge for the building's plumbing system. They flushed every toilet and turned on every sink at the same time. If the system could withstand that degree of activity, it could handle any gameday crowd.

The Friday before the grand opening, the team unveiled the Bob Feller statue outside of the center-field gates. The Indians hosted the Pittsburgh Pirates for an exhibition game the following afternoon. They were scheduled to hold an open house on Sunday afternoon, but Mother Nature interfered. They spent that day and Monday morning clearing snow from every seat as the clock ticked toward the first pitch of the new season.

And then, Opening Day 1994 arrived, the day on the calendar the Indians had circled for years; the day that, for decades, members of the organization only visualized in their most impractical dreams. Baerga referred to the new ballpark as a shiny, new toy. Alomar compared it to upgrading from a studio apartment to a sparkling, spacious new home.

"You didn't know exactly what it was going to look like, but you saw the steps," Lofton said. "You're like, 'Wow, this is going to be awesome.' And then, once you walked in there for the first time, when it was all set up, it was like, 'Wow.' That's when the excitement started to kick in. Damn, that old stadium was bad. We knew it was bad, but now seeing this new one, it was like, 'That was extremely bad.' It was like night and day. It was like a fantasy world, going from the old stadium to the new one."

Omar Vizquel recalled driving in on I-90 and laying his eyes upon the new architecture for the first time and feeling a bit intimidated.

"What it did for the city and the skyline, that part of downtown Cleveland," Nagy said, "it just changed everything."

Vizquel remembers playing at Tiger Stadium where, even though he barely stood 5'9", he had to duck down to avoid knocking his head on the ceiling in the visitors' dugout. He remembers playing at Old Comiskey in Chicago when it was decaying, and he heard tales about Candlestick Park in San Francisco and "what an ugly ballpark that was." So seeing Jacobs Field was a shock to his system.

"Nobody knew what to expect," Vizquel said. "Even though you see it in pictures and all that, you never expect it when you're walking in there, like, 'Wow. This is like Disneyland. This is beautiful.'"

And the amenities. Oh, what a 180.

"At the old ballpark, we would come to the ballpark late, maybe an hour before stretch," Baerga said. "At the new ballpark, we would come to the ballpark early. We could work out. We could go to the cages."

Said Lofton, "You didn't want to leave. Guys got to the ballpark at 1 o'clock for a 7 o'clock game just to hang out."

Folk noted that the entire home clubhouse—including the lockers, the toilets, the showers, the laundry station, and the equipment storage space—could have fit inside the new locker area at Jacobs Field. The reversal of conditions enticed some players to stick around once the season ended in the fall. Thome purchased a home in the suburbs. Alomar hung around in the winter.

"That was important," Folk said. "I think a lot of that played out in our success in the '90s. Players felt better about being in Cleveland. That whole attitude carried through."

Thome was grateful for the proximity of the batting cages to the dugout and the clubhouse. When he served as the designated hitter, he could take hacks while his teammates played the field.

"It was night and day," Sorrento said. "We didn't even have a food room in the first place. They put the spread out and that was it. Then all of a sudden you go from there to a kitchen and a chef and then you go from maybe a couple dumbbells to a state-of-the-art weight room. You go from one batting cage to five. It was the past and the future."

Every wall and carpet square appeared brighter. Every blade of grass carried a richer shade of green. Every room seemed spacious. The food tasted better. To some, even the bathrooms presented perks.

"You go into the bathroom and even the toilet looked better," Lofton said. "You felt like you could sit in there. You used to go into the bathroom before and get in and get out. Now, you're like, let me get the stats and read the stats while I'm in here for a while now. You felt like, 'Damn, this is cool to sit in here for a long time.' The other one was like, 'I gotta get up out of here real quick.'"

There were no more absent ceiling tiles in the offices, no more rodent hangouts. Team executives could sit at their desks without the need for a space heater or long johns.

"It was like Christmas," O'Dowd said. "Every single day showing up there was like Christmas Day. For us, it was that beautiful. It was that much of an upgrade."

And not only was the architecture upgraded, but so was the major league roster. The front office followed through on its plan to surround the young core with veteran complements, in the form of Dennis Martínez and Eddie Murray. Martínez, nicknamed El Presidente, had been one of the more steady right-handed workhorses in the league over the previous decade and a half. Even as he approached his 40th birthday, he could still chew up innings and limit walks and home runs. He made the National League All-Star team with the Montreal Expos in 1990, '91, and '92.

When the Indians signed Murray, one of the most accomplished hitters in the league, he stood 180 hits shy of the 3,000 mark. He

28

turned 38 about six weeks before Opening Day, but he had appeared in at least 150 games in each of the previous seven seasons, and in 11 of the previous 12. The Indians officially announced both free-agent deals on the same day in early December 1993. A couple of weeks later, they shipped shortstop Felix Fermin and first baseman Reggie Jefferson to the Seattle Mariners in exchange for Vizquel. They signed veteran catcher Tony Peña to serve as Alomar's backup.

"Everything was working," Shapiro said. "We were getting to be a good team. And the new stadium was that cultural energy resource. It was like this giant lift."

By the time Opening Day 1994 arrived, Folk was operating on a blend of adrenaline and coffee. Every concern ran through his mind. How does the weather forecast look? Are the lines for the bathroom and the concession stands a reasonable length? Is it possible we forgot something? Was President Bill Clinton, scheduled to throw out the first pitch, properly accommodated?

"You're sitting back, thinking, 'Okay, this has come to reality,'" DiBiasio said. "Herb Score opened up the broadcast with the line, 'It's very rare when you exceed expectations.' We all knew this was going to be new and beautiful and wonderful, this baseball-only, intimate setting. But it far exceeded anyone's expectations."

When fans entered the ballpark for the first time, they explored every square inch. If they had lower-level seats, they toured the upper deck. If they had nosebleed seats, they completed a lap or two around the main concourse. DiBiasio was amazed at how clean everyone wanted to keep the building. There were no wayward hot dog wrappers. Discarded peanut shells found their way into an empty cup. Worn-out bubble gum went in the trash can, not on the bottom of the seat.

Clinton, wearing an Indians starter jacket and a navy cap with a red bill and Block C, warmed up in the cages. Later that night, Arkansas would top Duke in the NCAA Tournament national championship basketball game. Nagy stirred up conversation about the game with Clinton, since he served as governor of Arkansas prior to winning the presidency.

"Everybody's telling him, 'Don't bounce it,'" Alomar said. "All he did was laugh. He went out there and did a good job."

A few years ago, Lofton and Clinton crossed paths in Lake Tahoe.

"Kenny Lofton! Do you remember when I threw that first pitch?" Clinton asked.

"Yeah, I remember," Lofton said. "I remember."

Clinton, Feller, and Ohio Governor George Voinovich each lofted a ceremonial first pitch to Alomar. Minutes later, Martínez tossed a strike for the first pitch of the season, the first official pitch at Jacobs Field. Alomar rolled the ball toward the dugout, a memento destined for a display case. The team stores it in its archives room at the ballpark.

"The sellout looked different than in the past," Alomar said. "It almost looked like, 'This is how it's going to be every day.'"

Lofton said he can remember every detail about the game "like it was yesterday." Even for those not in attendance, it was the sort of milestone event that never escapes the memory banks. Shapiro can remember watching the game at a Beef O'Brady's restaurant in Winter Haven, Florida, with longtime team advisor Johnny Goryl.

"The city, the fans, they started off the charts," Lofton said. "Everybody was trying to get tickets. It was like a sellout concert. Everybody wanted to be a part of that. It put chills back in your body, just being a part of it."

For those who had ever experienced a chilly day at the damp dungeon down the street, this change of pace was difficult to grasp.

"Before that," Sorrento said, "it was like playing at a legion game. You had girlfriends and wives there and friends, and that was about it. We went from about 5,000 a game to about 40,000. That was awesome."

O'Dowd: "I just crack up, because that's like walking from a starter home into a mansion. Not even a starter home. I can't describe to you how difficult that was, Municipal Stadium."

Folk: "You see the people coming in for the first time. The whistle would blow, the gates would open, and people would just come in and—fortunately, the concrete was all smooth and we didn't have too many tripping hazards, because they would all be looking up, just taking in this whole place, this brand new, beautiful, gleaming, unlike-anything-they-had-seen-before place."

So, imagine a sun-splashed spring afternoon in a vividly colored venue, a pristine ballpark home to a promising team poised to turn heads. Everything was perfect. The previous four decades of misery meant nothing. The Indians were ready to usher in a new era of baseball in the heart of downtown Cleveland.

The only thing standing in the way stood, well, 6'10", to be exact.

"I remember how the ballpark was alive," O'Dowd said. "I certainly remember that we had to face, of all guys, Randy Johnson, on Opening Day."

Ah, yes, the reigning AL strikeouts leader and Cy Young Award runner-up, the southpaw who set the league standard for fewest hits allowed per nine innings. Just the sort of slider-slinging machine a team wants to face on a brisk afternoon to begin its season.

"I was off that day, for probably good reasons, to be honest with you," Thome said. "Randy was one of the best left-handed pitchers."

And he carried a no-hitter into the eighth inning. That is one way to hush a jazzed-up sellout crowd.

Alomar spoiled Johnson's no-hit bid with an eighth-inning single, which followed a Candy Maldonado walk and a successful jinx attempt by Feller, who barged into the broadcast booth to openly acknowledge the hurler's attempt at history. Feller remains the only pitcher to record an Opening Day no-hitter.

After a wild pitch pushed both runners into scoring position, Ramirez socked a game-tying double to left field. Each team scored a run in the 10th inning. In the 11th, Wayne Kirby slapped a walk-off single to left to propel the Indians to a 4–3 victory.

O'Dowd: "That really set the tone for the season."

DiBiasio: "The most significant day, for sure."

Thome: "How that all unfolded, I think the magic kind of started from that."

Sorrento: "When you play in front of crowds like that, just the atmosphere shot life into everybody."

Baerga: "We were waiting for that. Now we had a place we could call our house. When everything is new, you see the ballgame in a different way. And everything changed. We had 455 nights in a row with that ballpark packed. It was amazing."

Thome: "The electricity was incredible. When the fans come out, you want to entertain. You want to do well for them. You want to live in that big moment. As a hitter, coming up in the ninth inning and having the fans support you, that raises your game to another level. What a great time to be in Cleveland. When we moved in from the old ballpark, it was a feeling like no other. And once we started to win, you could really see the city come alive."

It was the first signal that this team had some fight, that it could absorb a few punches and then claw back. It was the first execution of a walk-off celebration that would become customary. It was the first hint that hidden in the newly erected beams and pillars and concrete fixtures was a bit of magic.

Said Vizquel, "It was the beginning of a great history there for the Cleveland Indians."

3

"A Year of 'What If?'"

MARK WILEY REMEMBERS the first day of spring, when baseball after baseball soared beyond the outfield fence at Chain of Lakes Park. One player after another stepped into the batter's box and unloaded six months of pent-up frustration on a bucket of hapless baseballs, whacking every batting practice toss sent their way.

Albert Belle referred to 1994 as a "warmup season." The Indians arrived at spring training in Winter Haven, Florida, in April 1995 with an obvious sense of urgency and a palpable sense of confidence. The players had been sitting at home, waiting for the phone to ring, waiting some more for the phone to ring, and waiting some *more* for the phone to ring, as the strike persisted and threatened the 1995 season.

It began in 1994, just when the Indians had finally turned a corner and seemed poised to register the franchise's best single-season record since the pennant-winning 1954 team that racked up an unfathomable 111 victories. The Indians had spent a few weeks in first place in the newly formed American League Central Division in June and July, and as they reached the dog days of August, they trailed the White Sox by one game in the standings. They averaged a league-high 6.01 runs per game, and they logged the fifth-best team ERA in the AL. They scored at a higher rate than they would in 1995, and they ranked first in the AL in home runs and tied for first in batting average.

"We went out and went 76–86 [in 1992 and '93], but you really started seeing the thing come together as we went into the new ballpark," Dan O'Dowd said. "Everything just came together in a perfect storm. The talent on our team was overwhelming. Mixing that with an incredible environment, clubhouse, training, everything to put them in, it just all happened at the most opportune moment."

But the 1994 season produced one of the most inopportune moments in league history. The Indians were on the road—a four-game set at Fenway Park followed by a series north of the border in Toronto. They topped the Blue Jays 5–3 at the Skydome on the afternoon of Wednesday, August 10, as Jason Grimsley out-pitched Toronto's Juan Guzman. They wouldn't play again for more than eight months. A player's strike wiped out the postseason, the first year without a World Series since 1904.

"We were really devastated," O'Dowd said. "We didn't start out that year well. We went 14–17 out of the gate. Then we went 52–30 the rest of the time up until the strike. We were just hitting our stride. The White Sox were really formidable back then. We had a great rivalry going. I believe we had an opportunity to…"

O'Dowd paused, thinking about the club's potential that year.

"We were just getting better as the year went on, and we had a wave of talent that was coming."

No one knows how that season would have unfolded. Many have wondered whether the Expos, who boasted a league-best 74–40 record and an impressive collection of young talent—Pedro Martínez, Cliff Floyd, Larry Walker, Moises Alou, Marquis Grissom, Ken Hill, John Wetteland, Wil Cordero—could have captured the franchise's first championship and remained in Montreal long term. Instead, the

1994 campaign represents the only one of the franchise's 36 seasons in Montreal in which the Expos finished in first place. They started to sell off pieces the following spring, and ultimately relocated to Washington D.C. a decade later.

The Indians stood at 66–47, and the AL Central winner likely would have faced the AL West winner in the first round of the post-season. All four AL West teams were jockeying for division supremacy. That is not a compliment. The Rangers, at 52–62, led the pack the day the strike began. So, it's certainly possible that one of the AL Central teams (the Royals lurked behind the White Sox and Indians at 64–51) could have made some noise in the postseason, with the Yankees—powered by Wade Boggs and Paul O'Neill—providing the only legitimate competition.

Belle and Kenny Lofton finished third and fourth, respectively, in the AL MVP voting. Both produced ridiculous numbers in the 113-game season. Both players' batting average, on-base percentage, and slugging percentage were all career bests.

Belle: .357/.438/.714 slash line (1.152 OPS), 36 home runs, 101 RBIs, 90 runs, nine stolen bases.
Lofton: .349/.412/.536 slash line (.948 OPS), 12 home runs, 57 RBIs, 105 runs, 60 stolen bases.

Other teams were starting to take notice of Cleveland's collection of talent.

"They all seemed to click," Mike Hargrove said. "The main idea of it being that it was time to be where they were supposed to be. You get a sense of that, and then it gets reinforced, because in '94, I had a number of managers that heard other players say how good we were and how much better we could get. It was gratifying and satisfying to hear that from the teams that you played against, the managers you played against."

The strike certainly sucked the air out of the proverbial balloon. The Indians' momentum was halted, and a fan base that had started to gravitate toward its rising team in a new, state-of-the-art building, had to temper its excitement. In the days and weeks leading up to the work stoppage, fans had worn shirts and crafted signs begging the players and owners to set aside their differences and pinpoint some middle ground.

Everything was put on hold. Baseball really suffered. Though the strike started in mid-August, some players held out hope that the sides would reach an agreement in time to salvage the postseason. On September 14, though, Indians owner Dick Jacobs called general manager John Hart to inform him that the owners had voted to cancel the remainder of the season, including the playoffs. Hart exited his office and sat in the stands at Jacobs Field to reflect on the gravity of the situation. He could not believe how everything was unfolding.

Hart held a press conference that day, in which he said, "All we ever wanted to do since we started building this team in 1989 is to do what we've done this year. It hurts, especially the fans. And I think there's a little Indians fan in everyone in America."

Even if the 1994 season would not have served as their coronation, would some pennant race experience have benefited the Indians a year later, when they traversed the postseason for the first time as a group? We'll never know.

"It was an unbelievable breakout season for us," Sandy Alomar Jr. said, "although '94 was a year of 'What if?' We wanted to prove to people that '94 was not a fluke and that we had turned that corner as a team and that we knew how to finish games and be a championship-caliber team."

It was the most intrusive work stoppage the league had endured since 1981, when a strike cost teams two months of the regular season. This time, the strike lasted for 232 days. There was no baseball in September or October. A harsh winter followed. And when spring arrived, so did rosters full of replacement players in Florida and Arizona. The situation made everyone uneasy. The actual players were antsy, and not exactly thrilled with the non-union members who opted to attend spring training. Indians players could do nothing but twiddle their thumbs, sit around, jog on the treadmill, and wait for some news. Fans were disenchanted. Coaches felt uncomfortable. Everyone was waiting for a resolution.

It finally arrived on April 2, the day after the Indians and Mets played a sort of Bizarro World exhibition game at Jacobs Field (which was initially delayed by snow). Teams would have an abbreviated spring training and then the regular season would begin about three weeks later than originally intended. The regular season docket would be reduced to 144 games. Indians players couldn't care less; they just wanted to return to action, to build off of their 1994 uprising. The warmup season was in the rearview. They were ready for the real thing.

And they made that immediately evident.

"The most electric thing to me was the day they showed up after the replacement players were let go," said Wiley, the team's pitching coach. "I've never seen a batting practice like that, ever. We must have lost 1,000 balls. Those guys were so excited to be back. They were just hitting bombs everywhere. And it wasn't just our regular players. It was our Triple-A players, because we had good ones. We had guys like [Brian] Giles, [Jeromy] Burnitz, [Richie] Sexson, and guys like that in the minor leagues who were really good players. So from a coaching standpoint, we looked at it like, 'Man, we have some depth. We have some great players. This is our time.' It was absolutely off the charts."

Attendance and TV ratings across the league suffered in the aftermath of the strike, though you wouldn't know it judging by the appetite for winning baseball in Cleveland. All but three of the 28 teams—the Red Sox, Angels, and Indians—suffered attendance decreases from 1994 to '95. The Rangers lost more than 12,000 fans per game, and four other clubs lost at least 10,000 per home affair. Average attendance across the league plummeted from 31,240 fans per game in '94 to 25,048 per game in '95.

"What was unique about that season was we were living in a vacuum," Mark Shapiro said, "free from what everybody else in MLB was experiencing. Everyone else in MLB was inundated and over-whelmed with the negative sentiment and had a massive hangover that impacted their business. Everyone from our fans to our players to our front office was anxious to get back on the field and pick up where we left off, knowing we had a 40-year drought. Our revenues were not just good, they were amplified, and that's what led us to have payrolls in the top five in all of MLB, which was hard to imagine."

The Indians jetted to Texas for Opening Day against the Rangers on April 27. Think they were restless while waiting for the season to start? By the end of the third inning, they had scored nine runs. Belle, Eddie Murray, and Paul Sorrento all hit home runs in the early going. Manny Ramirez and Carlos Baerga tacked on solo shots later in the game. Their bats had apparently not accumulated any rust during the eight-month layoff.

"We had a really good team in '94," Paul Sorrento said. "We had just moved into the new stadium that year, so we just started selling out a lot and it was just a whole different atmosphere from the old stadium. A lot of guys were anxious to get back. It was really weird, because it was a tough time. At that time, it was really hard. We had lost a lot—the playoffs and the World Series the year before. That negotiation was really tough. But I think once we got in camp, we knew we were going to be pretty good. It was just a matter of everybody staying healthy. And we all did, pretty much. I think we were all anxious to get back after '94, just to see where we could end up."

4

"The Names Crawled to Where They Should Be"

AT HIS HOUSE, MIKE HARGROVE owns a couple of working scorecards from the 1994 season. On one, Jim Thome's name is scripted into the No. 8 spot in the starting lineup, with Manny Ramirez batting right behind him. On the other, those names are reversed, with Ramirez hitting eighth and Thome rounding out Hargrove's order.

Ramirez was still a rookie in 1994, with only a brief, rocky cameo from the previous year to his credit. Thome had played parts of three seasons in the majors, but he was still searching for his big-league footing. Hargrove preferred to bring along both players at a deliberate pace, so he structured the lineup with the two youngsters at the bottom. It's not as though the club was hurting for offense.

Albert Belle provided plenty of thump in the middle of the order. Kenny Lofton, Carlos Baerga, and Sandy Alomar made life miserable for opposing pitchers. Eventually, Thome and Ramirez worked their way up to the sixth and seventh spots in the lineup, where they remained for much of the 1995 season. The embarrassment of hitting riches made filling out that lineup card a simple task for the manager.

"I didn't have to assemble anything," Hargrove said. "I put the sheet right down on my desk and the names crawled to where they should be."

On their way to a 100-win season—despite a strike-shortened schedule, remember—the Indians out-slugged their opponents on a nightly basis. They led the American League in runs, hits, home runs, stolen bases, batting average, on-base percentage, slugging percentage, total bases, and number of nightmares suffered by opposing pitchers. Twelve players on the team recorded at least 150 at-bats. Of those, eight of them boasted a batting average of at least .300. Nine of them registered a slugging percentage higher than .450.

In about half of their games, they scored six or more runs. In nearly a quarter of their games, they scored nine or more runs. They topped out at 17 runs in a game, but on three occasions, they scored 14 runs. On four occasions, they scored 12 runs. On six occasions, they scored 11 runs. On five occasions, they scored 10 runs. By the end of the season, no one needed a vacation more than the scoreboard operator at Jacobs Field.

Somehow, they were held scoreless three times. Jack McDowell, who claimed the AL Cy Young Award two years prior, tossed a four-hit shutout on September 11 at Jacobs Field. He threw 144 pitches. On May 27, left-hander Al Leiter blanked the Tribe across 7⅔ innings. Six days later, he repeated the performance—another 7⅔ innings without allowing the Indians' mighty bats to make any noise.

Only two spots in the lineup showed the slightest signs of weakness. Tony Peña garnered the bulk of the playing time behind home plate as Sandy Alomar Jr. worked his way back from major knee surgery. Peña was 38 years old, his best days with the bat well behind him—plus, he was saving up his home run heroics for October… or something like that. Omar Vizquel did not hit for much power, but Hargrove appreciated the shortstop's ability to switch-hit, steal bases (he swiped 29, second on the team only to Kenny Lofton's 54) and advance runners, especially if Lofton reached base and snagged second.

Everyone else in Hargrove's batting order transformed baseballs into tattered, soulless spheres, seemingly shot out of a cannon toward the sun.

"It was really obvious that we had guys who fit certain areas of the lineup," Hargrove said.

Charlie Manuel, the hitting coach, kept the machine well-oiled, spending hours upon hours in the batting cages with Belle and Thome and Ramirez. His aim was to simplify the hitting process for the burgeoning stars, and it helped to have input from eventual Hall of Famers in Eddie Murray and Dave Winfield.

"Charlie Manuel was unbelievable, as far as being able to get these guys steady [and] being a good hitting coach," said Paul Shuey, who constantly marveled at the sluggers' hitting acumen as they talked shop on the dugout bench. "He would say, 'I could lay wood on a bullet if I can get my front foot down.' He just carried himself in such a manner where that confidence, that easy confidence, carried across."

And for opposing pitchers, it was customary to have confidence vanish. At no point could they catch their breath or throw any get-me-over fastballs. The coaching staff stressed patience at the plate.

"We used to wear out the starting pitchers by taking a lot of pitches and seeing a lot of pitches and fouling balls off with two strikes," Alomar said. "I felt like it put the starting pitcher in a bad place and the bullpen would have to come in early in the game. We did that, especially in a four-game series. You want to make sure the bullpen gets in the first game. So we had a plan."

Belle, Ramirez, and Thome all ranked in the top 25 in the majors in walks. Thome ranked fifth and Ramirez ranked seventh among all big-league hitters in pitches per plate appearance. Shuey can recall sitting in the dugout during a game and listening to Alomar and another hitter picking apart the opposing pitcher's throwing motion. They could tell what pitch was coming when he initiated his delivery.

"It was like, 'That's a changeup. Okay,'" Shuey said. "It's just that kind of pedigree."

And they capitalized with an offensive outburst.

"It's weird," Shuey said. "The more the years went on, I'm like, 'I'm going to have to face them at some point in time.' I ended up having to face Albert. He jumped me one time. I had decent luck with him. I finally had to face Thome. He hit a double off me. So, yeah, I think it's probably good that I didn't have to face them at the time."

This is how Hargrove typically assembled the Lineup of Dreams.

1. CF Kenny Lofton

Baerga: "Kenny Lofton is going to be a Hall of Famer one day. I'm telling you right now."

It all started at the top with Lofton, whom Hargrove described as "the prototypical leadoff hitter." The Indians acquired Lofton from the Astros in exchange for catcher Eddie Taubensee after the 1991 season. Lofton finished runner-up to Brewers shortstop Pat Listach in the AL Rookie of the Year balloting in 1992, which, years later, looks like quite the gaffe on the part of the voters.

> *Lofton: .285/.362/.365 slash line, five home runs, 66 stolen bases, 54 strikeouts, 5.8 WAR*
> *Listach: .290/.352/.349 slash line, one home run, 54 stolen bases, 124 strikeouts, 3.4 WAR*

And how did those two careers play out?

Lofton: 2,103 games, .299/.372/.423 slash line, 2,428 hits, 130 home runs, 622 stolen bases, 62.4 WAR
Listach: 503 games, .251/.316/.309 slash line, 444 hits, five home runs, 116 stolen bases, 1.5 WAR

Lofton emerged as a force in 1993, when he batted .325, reached base at a .408 clip, stole 70 bases, and pocketed the first of his four consecutive Gold Glove Awards. His 1994 season might have been the strongest of his career, though. He earned the first of his six consecutive trips to the All-Star Game. He hit .349, posted a career-best .948 OPS (on-base plus slugging percentage), stole 60 bases, hit 12 home runs, led the league with 160 hits—and produced those gaudy numbers before a strike halted the season in its tracks.

"Everybody was talking about the year that Albert had, and he was right behind Paul O'Neill for the Triple Crown," said Dan O'Dowd, "but Kenny Lofton was having the kind of year that—I think it cost Kenny Lofton the Hall of Fame his first time around. I think he's going to get in eventually, but I believe that Kenny, he had a chance to be the AL MVP that year. He might have stolen 100 bases. Even back then, with Rickey Henderson, that was almost unheard of to do. [Kenny] was simply dominating games on both sides of the ball, but no one remembers that or talks about that. I wonder, if that strike didn't happen, if Kenny did win the MVP that year, if the whole Hall of Fame situation for him would have changed. He was like a human highlight film. Kenny had this flair to him, this athleticism that was just starting to blossom."

In 1995, Lofton batted .310 with an .815 OPS. He swiped 54 bases, nearly one every other game. He led the league with 13 triples. He walked nearly as often as he struck out, a common theme throughout his 17-year big-league career. And he set the table for a lineup stocked with brazen, bloodthirsty sluggers. He was everything any manager would envision in the perfect leadoff hitter.

"I can't believe people don't talk about that guy more," pitching coach Mark Wiley said. "The guy was a .300 hitter. They always say a Hall of Fame guy is supposed to dominate his position for 10 years. I don't think anybody did it much better than he did for 10 years in center field."

2. SS Omar Vizquel

Baerga: "Omar Vizquel is going to be a Hall of Famer."

Terry Francona can recall watching Vizquel struggling to hit the ball out of the infield as a teenager in Venezuela. But by the time Vizquel called it a career, the shortstop had racked up 2,877 hits, four more than some hot dog–gobbling icon named Babe Ruth. Of course, Vizquel played for nearly a quarter of a century. But he never would have stuck around for so long, he says, if he had not learned to switch-hit.

Vizquel was naturally right-handed, but when he was 20—at the recommendation of former Mariners hitting instructor Bobby Tolan—he learned to hit lefty.

"I had never hit left-handed before," Vizquel said, "and it was kind of weird that I was risking my career by trying to make a switch."

He figured he could gain some extra hits by standing on the side of the batter's box that sits closer to first base, a novel concept. He could drop down a bunt and capitalize on his speed. Plus, he batted .213

with a .295 slugging percentage in A-ball in Wausau, Wisconsin, so what did he have to lose?

"Maybe if I would have been left-handed from the get-go," Vizquel said, "maybe I would have had 3,000 hits and we wouldn't have to go through this [Hall of Fame] process."

Everyone raved about Vizquel's defensive ability, especially his soft, quick hands. That skill originated in Caracas, where, as a kid, he would scoop up baseballs with his bare hand on a field covered in rocks. But when Vizquel became capable with the bat, he emerged as a player teams valued until he reached his mid-forties. He wound up recording several strong seasons at the plate, and one thing remained constant—he rarely struck out.

In 1995, Hargrove preferred penciling his name into the No. 2 spot in the lineup. That might not jibe with today's methods of structuring a batting order, in which managers are often encouraged to stack their most imposing hitters at the top, but Hargrove trusted Vizquel's instincts at the plate, especially hitting behind Lofton. Vizquel could always be counted on to put the ball in play.

3. 2B Carlos Baerga

How much did Baerga covet the 200-hit mark? He once ditched his hospital bed for a spot in Hargrove's batting order in the final series of the regular season, all for the chance to add to his hit total, which sat at 199. How long he had spent in the hospital is up for debate; Baerga claims he was bedridden for a week. Sandy Alomar Jr. contends the leg infection—suffered after he fouled a ball off his ankle—kept Baerga at the hospital for *only* three days.

But Baerga begged his way back onto the field for Game 160 at Cleveland Stadium on a Friday night in 1993. He went hitless in his first three trips to the plate. When he approached the batter's box for his last opportunity, he surveyed the defensive arrangement. The third baseman was playing far off the bag and the Indians had runners on first and second, so Baerga deposited a bunt down the baseline. He sprinted down the line, safely crossed first base, and crumpled to the ground in pain.

"We always talk about why Carlos ran so slow," Lofton quipped. "He swears he runs fast. When you run, you go forward. Carlos is the only guy in major league history that runs and he goes sideways."

Still, Baerga was able to leg out his 200th hit, reaching that mark for the second consecutive season. And then he exited for a pinch-runner. And then he returned to the hospital. He missed the final two games of the year.

"I had to get 200 hits," Baerga said.

Baerga averaged 180 hits per season from 1992 to '95, when he routinely hit third in Hargrove's lineup. He posted a .315 batting average and an .827 OPS in that span. In 1995, he struck out only 31 times (to go along with 35 walks). He made three American League All-Star teams. He became the first second baseman since Rogers Hornsby seven decades earlier to register back-to-back seasons with 200 hits, 20 home runs, 100 RBIs, and a .300 batting average.

On top of the stat lines, Hargrove appreciated Baerga's switch-hitting ability. On April 8, 1993, Baerga became the first player in big-league history to slug a home run from both sides of the plate in the same inning.

"We had Omar, who was phenomenal at short," Wiley said, "and we had Carlos Baerga, who was, at that time, breaking all of these offensive records for second basemen. Just a perfect mix."

4. LF Albert Belle

Baerga: "I talked to the people at the Hall of Fame, and he finished third in votes to be in the Hall of Fame by the veteran's committee, so he might be coming later on. And if he [had] stayed healthy, he would be a Hall of Famer."

Just when a pitcher navigated his way through the pesky top-third of the Indians' order, he arrived at the most daunting task possible: trying to conquer Belle.

"Just think about Thome and Manny coming up as the little guys," Shuey said, "and watching Albert come up in every clutch situation and get a hit. Like, every clutch situation. And if he didn't get a hit, stay out of his way."

No one was more prepared or more focused. No one could strike a non-strike with more oomph. Belle routinely launched shoulder-high pitches into the bleacher seats in left field or onto the picnic plaza beyond the center field fence.

"When I think of Albert, I think of an intense competitor, a driven person, a meticulous work ethic," Mark Shapiro said. "Mean. Just a tough guy. He was a reliable guy. He came to play every single day and then he was driven to put up and produce every day. You knew what you were going to get from Albert. This guy was going to be fueled to help us succeed and achieve his personal success. He was an incredibly productive and intimidating offensive performer."

Belle slugged 234 home runs in his six full seasons with the Indians, including a career-high and league-leading 50 in 1995. From 1994 to '96, he batted .325 with a 1.085 OPS, 134 home runs, 125 doubles, 335 runs scored, 375 RBIs, and nearly as many walks as strikeouts. He finished in the top three in AL MVP balloting in each season.

"If Albert would have stayed healthy his whole life," Wiley said, "he would have been a Hall of Famer."

Trying to Find a Weakness in the Indians' 1995 lineup

It might require some expert sleuth work, but there has to be a way to pinpoint some deficiency in the 1995 Indians' offensive attack. The Braves ultimately silenced Cleveland's bats, of course, but no other team could do so for the six months leading up to the World Series. The Indians' team batting average of .291 was the league's highest since the 1950 Red Sox, powered by Ted Williams and Dom DiMaggio, hit .302 as a club. So, let's throw on a detective's cape (they wear capes, right?) and solve this case. What was the key to shutting down Mike Hargrove's relentless run-scoring machine?

Indians at Jacobs Field: .293/.366/.483 slash line
Indians on the road: .288/.356/.475 slash line

Elite hitters can whack the baseball at any location. Albert Belle would have produced eye-opening numbers even if he split his games between the North Pole and the Bermuda Triangle. There is a reason the Indians ranked first in the league in home wins (54) and tied for first in the league, with Atlanta, in road wins (46).

Indians vs. right-handed pitchers: .293/.363/.494 slash line
  (26 percent better than league average)
Indians vs. left-handed pitchers: .285/.355/.440 slash line
  (10 percent better than league average)

Well, well. We have unearthed our first valuable piece of information, although it surely doesn't highlight any form of weakness. The Indians obliterated right-handed pitchers. The Indians only ravaged left-handed pitchers. Hargrove would often find at-bats for Herbert Perry and Alvaro Espinoza when a southpaw stood on the hill. For good reason, in Perry's case: the rookie corner infielder registered a .344/.403/.594 slash line against lefties. Perry also batted .296 against righties, just without the power (.378 slugging percentage).

Indians before the All-Star break: .292/.359/.491 slash line
Indians after the All-Star break: .289/.362/.468 slash line

Okay, so the midseason reprieve didn't cool them off or make them rusty. The Indians were just about as effective at the plate in the second half. In fact, the Indians' OPS by month: .826, .860, .844, .801, .836, .856. Didn't these guys ever get tired?

Indians in wins: .319/.387/.529 slash line
Indians in losses: .220/.293/.355 slash line

Aha! So, the key was...beat them. Yeah, this doesn't tell us much, other than, on the rare occasion the lineup didn't perform, the opposition at least had a chance to capitalize. Oh, and that first line explains how the Indians recorded 29 victories by five or more runs.

Indians when swinging at the first pitch: .374 average, .976 OPS
(29 percent better than league average)

All right, it clearly did not behoove pitchers to start at-bats with a pitch the hitter could punish. The only problem is, if a pitcher fell behind, the Indians would crush them.

Indians when swinging at a 1–0 pitch: .350 average, .951 OPS
Indians when swinging at a 2–0 pitch: .358 average, 1.042 OPS
Indians when swinging at a 3–0 pitch: .467 average, 1.906 OPS
Indians when swinging at a 2–1 pitch: .371 average, .987 OPS
Indians when swinging at a 3–1 pitch: .372 average, 1.296 OPS

Yeah, falling behind in the count was not a sound strategy.

Okay, okay, so maybe try to sneak in a first-pitch strike somehow, get ahead in the count, and then the pitcher controls the entire encounter, right? Right? (No. Not right.)

Indians when swinging at an 0–1 pitch: .313 average, .809 OPS

When swinging at an 0–2 pitch, Tribe hitters batted .189 with a .504 OPS, which might seem rough, but was still 69 percent better than league average, given the advantages a pitcher has in such a situation. When ahead in the count 0–2, a pitcher can waste a couple of pitches or try to entice a batter to chase a breaking ball out of the zone. Odds are not in the hitter's favor, though they were better if said hitter played for the '95 Indians.

Indians when batting with two outs: .283/.360/.453 slash line
Indians when batting with runners on base: .300/.371/.493 slash line
Indians when batting with runners in scoring position:
   .294/.374/.477 slash line
Indians when batting with runners in scoring position and two
   outs: .279/.371/.443 slash line

When they stepped up to the plate with runners aboard, it was reminiscent of a kid's eyes lighting up the moment he realizes his parent is pulling into the parking lot of the local ice cream parlor. And even with two outs, with pressure mounting and chances dwindling, the Indians still proved proficient.

Indians when ahead in the count: .285/.356/.474 slash line
Indians when behind in the count: .303/.358/.502 slash line
Indians in low-leverage situations: .278/.352/.454 slash line
Indians in high-leverage situations: .312/.379/.525 slash line

There's a reason bench coach Buddy Bell harped that the lineup fared better when the club was pushed around a bit. The

Indians, in a weird, masochistic kind of way, seemed to derive motivation from teetering on the edge of a loss. So, in the moments that mattered the most, they often performed the best.

Indians in the seventh inning: .244/.313/.398 slash line

Bingo! We found it! The seventh inning was the only one of the regular nine in which the Indians posted a team batting average below .271 or a team OPS below .777. Now, why the seventh inning? Who knows? This...doesn't seem too significant.

Indians vs. opponent with a winning record: .285/.347/.463 slash line
Indians vs. opponent with a losing record: .293/.367/.486 slash line

The Athletics were the only team to hold the Indians to an OPS below .750. Oh, and the Indians swept the season series against those Athletics, winning all seven games and outscoring them by a 34–17 margin. Congratulations to Oakland nonetheless.

Indians in night games: .293/.362/.487 slash line
Indians in day games: .286/.358/.461 slash line

No next-day hangovers here. The Indians were both solar- and lunar-powered.

Indians in open-air stadiums: .290/.361/.475 slash line
Indians in domes: .298/.353/.515 slash line

There was no use in placing an order for a retractable roof. The Indians piled up hits and runs whether playing indoors or outdoors.

The research clearly illustrates a few ways to silence the Indians' booming bats: only play the seventh inning of a game, make sure that it's a low-leverage situation, that there's a left-handed pitcher on the mound, and that every count starts with the batter in an 0–2 hole. Piece of cake.

5. DH Eddie Murray

Baerga: "Eddie Murray, Hall of Famer. Dave Winfield, Hall of Famer. [Murray] was a bench player for us that year."

Shuey has fond recollections of his days in the Indians' dugout. He would finish his inning on the mound and then sit on the bench while his teammates smacked around the opposing pitcher. The Indians might as well have installed a few hammocks in the dugout for pitchers to relax and sip lemonade while the offense completed the heavy lifting.

Shuey can recall sitting between Murray and Winfield—a pair of hitters who combined for 6,365 hits over 43 major league seasons—during a game. Murray and Winfield dissected each hitter's approach and identified how best to capitalize on a pitcher's mistakes. Shuey listened intently to the conversation and applied the insight to his own gameplan.

"I think I went off and pitched great for two weeks," Shuey said, "because I'm like, 'Oh, he's moving up in the box. He's looking for this. He's doing this.'

"The knowledge—Eddie was so, so great."

Even at the age of 39, Murray produced a .323 batting average and an .891 OPS. By that juncture of his career, Murray had made eight All-Star teams and had finished in the top five in MVP voting on six occasions.

He typically served as the Indians' designated hitter, and Shuey marveled at the way Murray watched and processed the game during all his down time in the dugout. One time, he noticed Orioles right-hander Alan Mills dictating signs to his catcher before each pitch. Murray solved the riddle rather quickly and knew what Mills would throw.

"And then he could kill him," Shuey said. "The way he thought about the game, the way the whole group was able to think about the game—you had individuals like that, older veteran guys who had an incredible amount of experience, and to have all of that in one dugout, it was over the top.

"I just tried to keep big ears and a little mouth."

The Indians are the only franchise to employ three players who each reached the 3,000-hit milestone with the club. Nap Lajoie and Tris Speaker accomplished the feat during the presidencies of Woodrow Wilson and Calvin Coolidge, respectively. Murray—Bill Clinton had taken office by this point—yanked an outside offering from Twins righty Mike Trombley through the right side of the astroturf at the Metrodome for base knock No. 3,000 on June 30, 1995. Second baseman Chuck Knoblauch performed an unfruitful bellyflop in an effort to corral the sharp grounder. Murray rounded first base and slapped hands with coach Dave Nelson.

Murray's teammates spilled out of the visitors' dugout and swarmed him near first base for some congratulatory handshakes. The first-ballot Hall of Famer lifted his helmet and his cap—yeah, he wore both when batting—and acknowledged those in attendance who applauded the historic moment. He became the 20th player in major league history to collect his 3,000th hit.

6. 3B Jim Thome

Baerga: "Thome is a Hall of Famer."

In 2018, the box beside Thome's name was checked by 379 of 422 Hall of Fame voters. In 1995, Thome launched that Cooperstown campaign. He had played regularly for the first time the year before, though Hargrove still tended to shy away from the left-handed slugger when the Indians faced a southpaw starter. In 1995, Hargrove removed the training wheels.

"I tried to bring [Thome and Ramirez] along slowly, but in '95, it was just everybody fit in the lineup where they were supposed to fit. It was a good job."

Thome typically batted sixth against a right-handed starter, and seventh or eighth against a lefty. And this was a guy who posted a .314/.438/.558 slash line in 1995. He walked 97 times, and he totaled 29 doubles and 25 home runs. That home run count was his lowest until an injury-plagued 2005 season.

Thome eventually became the Indians' all-time home run leader, with 337. In 1995, he and Ramirez were the talented kids in a lineup filled with veterans.

7. RF Manny Ramirez

Baerga: "Without what happened to Manny, he would be in the Hall of Fame."

Ramirez's smooth, right-handed stroke produced 555 home runs, a .312 average, and a .996 OPS across 19 major league seasons. Perhaps no game showcased his two most prevailing traits—power and, um, ditziness—more than a contest at a mostly deserted Yankee Stadium on September 3, 1993, Ramirez's second career game.

Ramirez struck a rising heater from Melido Perez toward the blue wall in left field in the second inning. The ball caromed off the warning track and disappeared into the seats. Ramirez trotted around first base and cruised toward second after he notched a ground-rule double for his first big-league hit. Only Ramirez thought he had clubbed a home run. So he breezed past second base and continued on, without hesitation, to third. Jeff Newman, the third base coach, directed him back to second, but not before Ramirez's teammates in the visitors' dugout erupted in laughter. Candy Maldonado raised two fingers to remind Ramirez that a ground-rule double rewards a hitter with two bases, not four. Baerga raised both arms to urge Ramirez to stop his leisurely jog.

Though the ballpark was largely abandoned, Ramirez did have a raucous contingent of family and friends in the crowd. He attended George Washington High School in Manhattan, a couple miles from Yankee Stadium. In the sixth inning, Ramirez launched a Perez offering into the left-field stands. This time, he could stroll around the bases at his own pace and proceed until he returned to the dugout. He tacked on another home run two innings later to finish his second career game with three extra-base hits.

Ramirez's actions regularly sparked laughter in the dugout and the clubhouse. In 1994, as the Indians watched the video of O.J. Simpson's infamous highway chase, Ramirez actually thought the TV news bulletin was highlighting his teammate in the white Ford Bronco. Yes—he thought the Los Angeles police were pursuing [Chad] Ogea, not O.J. [Simpson]. Ramirez often kept his paychecks in his glove compartment—without cashing or depositing them. Once, he and Julian Tavarez asked two Indians beat writers if the players could each borrow $10,000 to buy a motorcycle. The reporters, stunned and confused, laughed and denied their request, before asking the players if they had any idea what sort of salary a baseball writer earned.

Ramirez finished second in the balloting for AL Rookie of the Year in 1994. The 1995 campaign was his first full season, and he made the All-Star team (his first of 12 trips to the Midsummer Classic), compiled a .308/.402/.558 slash line, and belted 31 home runs. He also captured the first of his nine Silver Slugger awards and he participated in the Home Run Derby. His Hall of Fame chances ultimately fizzled because of his positive tests for performance-enhancing drugs, but in 1995, he was a sweet-swinging 23-year-old who produced All-Star numbers from the lower part of the Indians' lineup.

"You had Manny and Thome hitting sixth and seventh, seventh and eighth, something like that," Lofton said. "The numbers they eventually put up when they were on that team, that low in the lineup—any other team, they would be hitting third and fourth. On that team, they were hitting sixth and seventh."

8. 1B Paul Sorrento

The Angels selected Sorrento in the fourth round of the 1986 amateur draft and then traded him two years later to the Twins for Bert Blyleven, a two-time All-Star and eventual Hall of Fame inductee with 287 wins to his name. In 1991, Sorrento and the Twins won the World Series. And then, five months later, Minnesota dealt him to the rebuilding Indians for a couple of relief prospects.

Sorrento manned first base while suffering through a couple of losing seasons with Cleveland in 1992 and '93. He typically batted fifth, sometimes sixth. And then the Indians' lineup got stronger (and younger) and Sorrento often found himself slotted into the No. 7 or No. 8 spot in Hargrove's order, even though he batted .280 in 1994 and hit 25 home runs and tallied 79 RBIs in only 104 games in '95.

"There were always guys on base, it seemed like, when you came up," Sorrento said. "We were tough outs. We were really tough outs. We created a lot of runs that way. It was a different guy every single day. It was one through nine, for sure. It didn't let up."

"That takes the pressure off of everybody. Guys knew that they didn't have to do it every night. Obviously, as a player, you want to. But the reality of it is, you're not going to. So it was a pretty special lineup."

Sorrento posted an .847 OPS in 1995. In 280 at-bats against right-handed pitchers, he clubbed 23 home runs.

"We were loaded with talent," he said. "We had really good pitching and then some days, we would score 10 runs quick. It was crazy. Everybody had—I don't want to say career years, but everybody had a good year. A lot of guys in their prime. A really good mix of players. It was different every day. It was a pretty special year."

9. C Sandy Alomar Jr.

Baerga: "I always say, if Sandy wasn't hurt that much, he would have put up some unbelievable numbers, maybe enough to be a Hall of Famer."

Hargrove planned for Alomar to receive a couple of at-bats on the final day of the regular season in 1995. Alomar, who missed the first half of the season following knee surgery, played a lot in August (26 games) but received more rest in September (only 18 games). Alomar entered Game 144 with a .288 batting average, the result of him collecting six hits in 12 at-bats over his previous four games.

"I wasn't even thinking about hitting .300," Alomar said. "I just said, 'Let me finish good.' My whole thing was to come in strong and finish solid."

Well, the first eight batters of the game reached via a single or a walk. Alomar, the No. 9 hitter, flied out to center. He singled in the second. And again in the fourth. His batting average gradually crept toward the coveted .300 mark.

"We started calling up to the press box, asking, 'What am I hitting now?'" Alomar said. "'299 point what?'"

The Indians were obliterating the Royals, but Alomar convinced Hargrove to grant him another at-bat. He collected another single in the fifth. Alomar had one last shot in the eighth. Jesse Levis would be replacing him after his fifth and final trip to the plate. Alomar's average sat at .297, but a base hit would vault it to .300, to be forever etched onto the back of his baseball card.

Alomar socked another single, this one to right field, his fourth base knock of the game. Levis trotted out to first base to pinch run.

"It was fun," Alomar said. "When you don't try to do too much, it happens. I wasn't expecting to hit .300. I was just going out there. But it was a good personal accomplishment."

Alomar's final slash line: .300/.332/.478. Not bad for a guy who was expected to miss the season after his knee operation. And not bad for a team's No. 9 hitter.

* * *

So, that's the Hargrove Special, Murderer's Row reincarnated. The Indians scored 39 more runs than any other team in the majors. They struck out fewer times than any other team in the majors. Thome, Belle, and Ramirez, the muscle in the middle of the order, proceeded to occupy the top three spots on the Indians' all-time home run list.

"I haven't seen a lineup like that in I don't know how long," Lofton said. "We haven't seen it to that effect. We led offensive categories that were off the charts, to this day.

"What was it, seven out of the nine guys were hitting at least .300, something like that?"

(That is correct.)

"I always just felt like every time I got on base, there was an 80 percent chance I was going to score. That's a high percentage for scoring runs. I tried to get in scoring position, because I knew if I got on base and put myself in scoring position, those guys were going to put the ball in play. They weren't going to just strike out. That wasn't their motto. Their motto was to put it in play."

Five Most Impressive Hitting Performances of the 1995 Regular Season

During the 1995 season, the Indians had a player hit multiple home runs in a game on 20 occasions. Albert Belle was responsible for eight of those. Seven other players also accomplished the feat. (Worthless trivia: Herbert Perry hit three home runs all year, but two came in the same game.) There were 19 instances of a Tribe hitter collecting at least four hits in a game. There were 15 occurrences in which a Cleveland player drove in four or more runs in a single contest.

But who authored the most impressive single-game performances at the plate in 1995? Let's examine five that stand tall.

Eddie Murray: May 7 against the Twins at Jacobs Field

The stat line: 4-for-5 with two home runs, two singles, a walk, and a stolen base

Murray racked up four hits, including two home runs, and he watched the final five innings of the Indians' 10–9 victory from the dugout bench. Seventeen-inning affairs don't pop up too often. Murray certainly made the most of his time on the field, though. He handed the Indians a 1–0 lead in the first inning with an RBI single, broke a 2–2 deadlock with a three-run blast in the third, singled and swiped second base in the fourth, and answered Marty Cordova's go-ahead homer minutes earlier with a game-tying solo shot of his own in the bottom of the eighth. Murray walked in the 12th inning and was replaced on the bases by Ruben Amaro. So, he sat back and waited...and waited...and waited...until the Indians emerged victorious in the 17th inning. Murray's win probability added, an advanced statistic that measures a player's contributions and how they influence a game's outcome, was .553, one of the highest marks any Indians player produced in 1995, even more

68

impressive considering Murray wasn't in the game to deliver the decisive hit.

Albert Belle: September 19 against the White Sox at Comiskey Park

The stat line: 3-for-4 with three solo home runs and a walk

With runners on second and third and one out in the top of the first—thanks to a Kenny Lofton steal and a Lofton/Carlos Baerga double steal—the White Sox opted to intentionally walk Belle to load the bases. They refused to allow Belle to drive in those two runs, but they scored later in the inning anyway. And, well, perhaps the White Sox should have issued Belle a free pass every time he stepped into the batter's box. Belle led off the sixth with a solo home run. Belle led off the eighth with a solo home run. Belle led off the ninth with a solo home run. He made victims of three different pitchers: Luis Andujar, Scott Radinsky, and Rod Bolton. The Indians won 8–2.

Oh, and Belle had socked two home runs the night before, too. Those torrid two days boosted his season home run total to 44 with nine games remaining. He would come up empty over his next two games, and then club five more in a three-game stretch.

So, is it more impressive to say he hit 10 home runs in a seven-game span, or to say he hit 12 home runs in a 10-game span? Either way, Belle enjoyed a monster September, highlighted by the Indians' first three-homer game since Jim Thome turned the trick 14 months earlier.

Paul Sorrento: May 3 against the Tigers at Tiger Stadium

The stat line: 3-for-4 with a home run, two doubles, a sacrifice fly, and six RBIs

Sorrento made the most of his first two trips to the plate. In the second inning, he hit a two-run double to right-center field. In the third inning, he belted a three-run homer to right-center field. He added a sacrifice fly and another double later in the game. His six RBIs were the most by any Tribe hitter in a game all season.

The Indians pounded the Tigers 14–7 to move to 4–2 on the season. In those first six games, they piled up 57 runs, a ridiculous average of 9.5 per game. They also averaged more than 13 hits per game during that stretch, with at least 10 in every contest.

Kenny Lofton: September 13 against the Yankees at Jacobs Field

The stat line: 2-for-3 with a single, a double, two walks, two runs, and three stolen bases

Imagine how David Cone felt when, after 11 pitches, Lofton was standing on third base, despite no one putting the ball in play. Lofton led off the first inning with a walk. Two pitches later, he stole second. Two pitches after that, he stole third. One pitch after that, Vizquel grounded an RBI double to right and the Indians claimed the lead. Lofton batted again in the second, and he beat out an infield single. Five pitches later, with Vizquel at the plate, Lofton stole second. He couldn't steal third this time, since Tony Peña was standing on it. Lofton walked in the fourth and he doubled and scored in the sixth, as the Indians blanked the Yankees 5–0 behind Charles Nagy's complete-game shutout.

Lofton led the American League in stolen bases each year from 1992 to '96 (66, 70, 60, 54, 75). He swiped three bases in a game on 19 occasions in his career, though only once in 1995. He stole a career-high five in a game on September 3, 2000, when he also clubbed a walk-off home run.

Carlos Baerga: July 16 against the Athletics at Jacobs Field

The stat line: 5-for-6 with four singles and a double

This game is well-known for how it ended—on a Ramirez walk-off blast to the left-field bleachers—but Baerga notched the Indians' only five-hit game of the season to set the stage for Ramirez's heroics. The Indians trailed 3–1 in the seventh, when Baerga singled and scored on Belle's game-tying home run to left-center. With the game still tied in the ninth, Baerga singled and attempted to score on Belle's double to left, but Rickey Henderson nabbed Baerga at the plate. So Baerga started yet another rally in the 12th. The Indians had fallen behind 4–3 as Henderson used his wheels to manufacture a run against Alan Embree. Baerga collected his fifth hit of the game, a single to left, to set the comeback in motion. Three batters later, Ramirez launched a Dennis Eckersley offering toward the sun.

5

"Man, He Would Be a Great Closer ...I Think"

PAUL ASSENMACHER HAD COMPLETED his warm-up tosses. He was ready to ditch the visitors bullpen at Fenway Park and trot to the mound. As Mo Vaughn—the burly, left-handed hitter with power, a thick goatee and a hunchback-like batting stance—approached the plate in the bottom of the ninth, Mike Hargrove glanced at his pitching coach, Mark Wiley.

"What do you think?" Hargrove asked.

"If you want a closer," Wiley replied, "you have to let him close it." Hargrove agreed.

The Indians arrived at spring training without a strict plan for their closer role. Jose Mesa, the guy with the lively right arm and the handlebar mustache, had prepared for the job during winter ball in the Dominican Republic, but the Indians started the year without being married to that solution. Mesa was the default choice, but if the situation called for a lefty, they could turn to Assenmacher. If Julian Tavarez or Eric Plunk were in a groove, there was nothing preventing them from pitching the ninth.

This, though—the Indians' 20th game of the season—seemed like an opportune time for the coaching staff to challenge Mesa, to see if he could handle a high-leverage situation in a difficult environment and against an imposing hitter, who just so happened to win the American League Most Valuable Player award that season. (Never mind the fact that Albert Belle registered more impressive numbers in just about every single statistical category; Vaughn was still a daunting figure for any pitcher to face.)

Vaughn represented the tying run, as the Indians gripped a 7–5 lead in the ninth. Mesa had retired Luis Alicea and Troy O'Leary before John Valentin singled to left. Mesa was a converted (okay, perhaps "failed" is the more appropriate word) starter. He had too high of a walk rate and hit rate and too low of a strikeout rate to consistently pitch deep into games and wiggle out of harm's way. He fizzled out in Baltimore and the Orioles dumped him on the Indians in the middle of the 1992 season. Sandy Alomar Jr. can recall Mesa having no trouble breezing through three or four innings. But, well…

"That's about when the wheels would start to fall off," Alomar said.

Alomar remembers a conversation he had with general manager John Hart, in which Hart asked the catcher, "What's going on with this guy?"

"Man, he would be a great closer," Alomar told him, before backing off just a tad. "I think."

Hart considered the idea, saying, "We're going to have to try to do that. He just can't sustain for more than four innings."

In 1994, Mesa shifted to the bullpen and posted a 3.82 ERA. His numbers improved across the board. He had no prior experience with the closer role, though. Sure, it's just another three outs to record, but pitchers will tell you that traversing the ninth inning requires a certain mentality, a particular degree of fearlessness and a short memory.

The Indians had no evidence that Mesa could handle such pressure. They had to test him out in the role. So the bullpen phone never buzzed. Assenmacher remained a spectator. Mesa stayed on the mound. Vaughn entered the batter's box.

And Hargrove and Wiley each held their breath.

The count reached 2–2. On the fifth pitch of the encounter, Mesa pumped a high fastball past the eager slugger. Mesa pumped his right fist and shook hands with Tony Peña and Jim Thome.

As the coaches spilled out of the dugout, Wiley looked at Hargrove and said, "Well, we have ourselves a closer now."

"He had to experience that to show whether he could do it or not," Wiley said. "It was early in the season, so it would have been logical to say, 'Well, we'll go with a committee for a while until we find a better opportunity.' We could have hidden him in there with a three-run lead or something. But I'll never forget him getting Mo Vaughn out, who ended up being the MVP that year. That was when he really turned it on. He threw strikes and he attacked the strike zone.

"The rest was history that year."

Wiley marveled at the way Mesa stifled the first hitter of an inning. He held them to seven hits in 60 at-bats, and a .117/.145/.183 slash line (.328 OPS). With runners in scoring position, Mesa dug deep, limiting the opposition to a .125/.228/.208 slash line.

"He was always one pitch away from a double play if he was in trouble," Wiley said, noting Mesa's heavy, sinking fastball.

Mesa logged a 1.13 ERA for the season. He allowed one earned run in June, one unearned run in July, one earned run in August, and one earned run in September. He yielded only one earned run at Jacobs Field all season.

"He comes in as a closer and it was like he was there for years," Alomar said.

Mesa converted his first 38 save chances before the Tigers spoiled his streak in late August. Detroit got to him again a week later. No matter, since the Indians emerged victorious in both games.

Messing with Mesa

Long before their friendship turned sour, before Omar Vizquel criticized Jose Mesa's 1997 World Series performance in his autobiography and before Mesa retaliated by attempting to plunk the shortstop every time the two squared off on the diamond, the two had a tight bond. They had adjacent lockers in the Indians' clubhouse. They lived about five minutes apart in the suburbs on the west side of Cleveland. They hung out together. They cooked meals together.

One time, Vizquel and Carlos Baerga visited Sea World, and Vizquel purchased a miniature T-Rex figure. He placed it in Mesa's locker and when the reliever first saw it, his teammates made a high-pitched shriek, which startled him and triggered his temper.

"That was the worst thing we could have done," Baerga said. "That guy wanted to kill everybody, especially Omar."

During Mesa's seventh season with the Indians, the club traded him to San Francisco as part of a package that included Shawon Dunston and Alvin Morman. In exchange, the Indians landed outfielder Jacob Cruz and reliever Steve Reed. Mesa entered the free-agent market that winter and signed with Seattle, returning to the American League. So when the Mariners traveled to Cleveland and Mesa was summoned from the bullpen, Vizquel stood atop the dugout steps and made that same shrieking noise.

"I said, 'Omar, I don't think he's very happy about that,'" said Sandy Alomar Jr. "Then when he came up, the next pitch was behind him. He wasn't joking."

"Guys just happened to catch a fastball and hit it to the opposite field and then we won the game in the next bottom half of the inning anyway," Wiley said. "He almost had a flawless year. But it had a lot to do with Tavarez and Plunk and Assenmacher and Jim Poole and our main core of guys in the 'pen who were so consistent, we could count on them day in and day out."

Closers often tend to walk a tightrope; to make teammates, coaches, and fans uneasy; to convince any non-smoker to reach for the nearest pack of Marlboros. Ever sit on the runway long enough before takeoff that it jeopardizes whether you'll make your connecting flight in the next city so you spend the entire first flight agonizing over whether you'll have enough time to wait for every passenger in front of you to exit the plane and then sprint to your next gate, and you attempt to calculate, over and over and over in your head, precisely how many anxiety-ridden minutes you'll have before they slam the door shut? Many closers wind their way into messy jams that leave fans hunched forward on their couches, forehead buried in one hand, the other hand counting all the miracles it would require to preserve a one-run lead with the bases loaded and no outs.

In 1995, Mesa was the rare case of a closer who did no harm to his manager's blood pressure or his fan base's healthy habits. He racked up a league-high 46 saves. He finished second in the AL Cy Young Award voting, behind Randy Johnson, and fourth in the AL MVP balloting, behind Vaughn, Belle, and Edgar Martínez. (Again, the '95 AL MVP voting was such a mess.)

"Players are the ones who turn managers and coaches into geniuses," Wiley said. "You put them in the roles for an opportunity and they perform, and they make everybody look good. It always looks like the right decision. And in that case in that year, it was unbelievable how consistent those guys were. One day, Plunk would throw two innings. So the next day, we wouldn't use him. We would use Tavarez. And he would go two innings, or an inning and two-thirds. And we would use Assenmacher and those guys. We didn't have any catastrophes. And we also were very injury-free. Other than Sandy, of our core players, he was the only one that was injured that year for an exorbitant amount of time. Everybody else was healthy. Our pitching staff was healthy the whole year."

Mesa wasn't the only Tribe reliever to enjoy a career year in 1995. Tavarez recorded a 2.44 ERA and covered 85 innings. Assenmacher, who registered a 2.82 ERA, silenced lefties to the tune of a .188 batting average and a .470 OPS. Plunk posted a 2.67 ERA, with 71 strikeouts in 64 innings, his third consecutive season with a sub-3.00 ERA. He was even better in 1996.

"Our bullpen wasn't overused, either," Wiley said. "None of the guys had 70 or 80 appearances. Obviously, we played 18 games fewer than we normally would have. But if you look at the deal, Jose was the only reliever who really only threw one inning per outing. The rest of the guys, they could throw multiple innings. The health and the quality of the guys that we had, it just fit. It just fit like perfect. I can't think of it being any better."

A moment for some Plunk appreciation: he had his struggles for the Indians during the postseason. In fact, it was pretty ugly. In 12⅓ innings from 1995 to '97, he allowed 13 runs (12 earned) on 11 hits and 10 walks, for an 8.76 ERA. Once, his unsightly performance resulted in a 72-point-font newspaper headline the next morning that simply read: KER-PLUNK! However, in seven seasons with the Indians, Plunk posted a

3.25 ERA, with just about one strikeout per inning. He was incredibly consistent from 1992 to '96:

1992: 71 innings, 61 hits allowed, 29 earned runs allowed, 38 walks, 50 strikeouts

1993: 71 innings, 61 hits allowed, 22 earned runs allowed, 30 walks, 77 strikeouts

1994: 71 innings, 61 hits allowed, 20 earned runs allowed, 37 walks, 73 strikeouts

1995: 64 innings, 48 hits allowed, 19 earned runs allowed, 27 walks, 71 strikeouts

1996: 77 innings, 56 hits allowed, 21 earned runs allowed, 34 walks, 85 strikeouts

Thank you for attending this abbreviated Eric Plunk TED Talk.

The Indians signed Assenmacher about a week after spring training commenced, and less than three weeks before the start of the delayed regular season. He had proved to be a reliable relief option for the Braves, Cubs, Yankees, and White Sox for nearly a decade, and he had enough bullets in his left arm and enough fuel to power his high leg kick that he provided the Indians with four years of quality results before the bottom fell out in 1999. Assenmacher often entered in the late innings to hush the loudest left-handed bat on the opposing team. From 1995 to '98, he registered ERAs of 2.82, 3.09, 2.94, and 3.26, and he averaged a strikeout per inning. In those four years, he maintained a low walk rate and he surrendered only 14 home runs in 181 innings.

Tavarez signed with the Indians a couple of months shy of his 17th birthday, and he debuted in 1993 as a 20-year-old starting pitcher. By 1995, he was a reliever who could throw multiple innings. His durability granted Hargrove and Wiley the ability to use him on back-to-back days or for one extended appearance. He threw as many as 64 pitches in a single relief outing, and he also pitched on consecutive days on nine occasions. He put out fires in the late innings. He bridged the gap to Mesa in the ninth. He saved his fellow relievers by covering several innings in lopsided affairs. He did it all, and his super-reliever role—and the 2.44 ERA—earned him a tie for sixth place in the balloting for AL Rookie of the Year.

The Indians led the AL in bullpen ERA in 1995, and it wasn't even all that close.

1. Indians (3.05)
2. Angels (3.65)
3. Mariners (4.05)
4. Athletics (4.34)
5. Red Sox (4.37)

Having a lights-out bullpen can make life easier for the starting rotation, too.

"I don't think people knew as much about the bullpen," Wiley said. "We were one of the teams that turned it into a six-inning game and we had guys like Tavarez and Plunk and people like that who could go a couple innings and bridge to Jose Mesa."

Wiley served as a special assistant for the front office in 1993 and '94. He traveled across the country and evaluated certain players, including veterans who were bound to reach free agency right at the time the Indians wanted to add some experience to their young, burgeoning roster. He scouted Eddie Murray, whom the Indians ended up sticking in the middle of their lineup, the perfect, switch-hitting supporter to bat behind Albert Belle. Wiley also watched plenty of Orel Hershiser and Dennis Martínez "to see how much tread was still left on them."

The Indians introduced Murray and Martínez at the same press conference, on December 2, 1993. When Martínez took the hill on Opening Day in 1994, the christening of Jacobs Field, he stood a month shy of his 40th birthday. But the Indians were confident he could still lead the staff, and he earned a trip to the All-Star Game in 1995. Martínez finished that season with a 3.08 ERA across 187 innings.

Hershiser spent the first 12 seasons of his big-league career with the Dodgers. He was named to three All-Star teams. In 1988, he won the National League Cy Young Award and claimed World Series MVP honors, as he notched a pair of complete-game victories against the Athletics. Hershiser hit the free-agent market after the strike-shortened season in 1994, and he wanted to remain with Los Angeles, but the Dodgers moved in a different direction, as they inked Japanese star Hideo Nomo to a contract.

Hershiser contended he had discovered the fountain of youth in his mid-thirties, that he still had some juice in his right shoulder, which had been surgically repaired earlier in the decade. At the start of spring training, spurned by the Dodgers, Hershiser signed a three-year pact with the Indians. In those three seasons, Hershiser logged a 4.21 ERA and chewed up 568 innings for Cleveland. The '95 campaign was his best of the three, as he posted a 3.87 ERA in the regular season and a 1.53 ERA in five postseason starts, with 35 strikeouts in 35⅓ innings and an opposing batting average of .160.

Martínez and Hershiser anchored the rotation and imparted their wisdom upon younger starters, such as Charles Nagy and Chad Ogea.

"For me, it was the experience and the professionalism, knowing how to take care of themselves, knowing how to limit big innings," Wiley said. "They knew that our bullpen was strong as we got into the season and they knew that their job was, primarily, if you can get through six, we have a good chance of winning the game. They were focused from the first pitch on. I think the impact of the professionalism and showing the young guys how to pitch out of trouble was a big factor."

The Indians' starters did lead the league in strand rate (71.5 percent). They bent, but they didn't often break. They also led the AL in ERA (4.21) and walks per nine innings (2.9) and ranked second in home runs allowed per nine innings (0.98).

Nagy was a homegrown talent, selected in the first round of the 1988 amateur draft. He spent all but about 10 minutes of his career with the Indians, and he finished sixth in the AL Cy Young Award balloting in 1995.

"He was another big third cog with those other two guys," Wiley said.

To solidify the rotation, the Indians swung a deal with the Cardinals for veteran right-hander Ken Hill in late July. The Indians parted with three players, including young infielder David Bell, the son of the club's bench coach, Buddy Bell. It required some nitpicking to find an area of the roster that needed a midseason upgrade. The bullpen was a well-oiled machine. The lineup was a high-powered assembly line. The starting rotation was faring well, but the front office sought to augment the group's depth. Enter Hill, an All-Star and the NL Cy Young Award runner-up in 1994 with the upstart Expos. Montreal dealt him to St. Louis in an effort to trim payroll before the '95 season, a disheartening development eight months after the player's strike cut short their impressive bid to make some postseason noise.

The Cardinals were languishing in the NL Central basement en route to the second-worst record in the NL. They had fired manager Joe Torre a month earlier. Hill was bound for free agency at the end of the season anyway, so St. Louis granted him the opportunity to transition from a dreary situation into the thick of a pennant race. And lo and behold, Hill's numbers perked up following the midseason trade to Cleveland.

Hill with St. Louis: 5.06 ERA, 10.2 H/9, 1.3 HR/9, 4.1 K/9
Hill with Cleveland: 3.98 ERA, 9.3 H/9, 0.6 HR/9, 5.8 K/9

"Hill had been struggling," Wiley said, "and we spotted some mechanical things we thought we could fix.... He was a big help to us, too. It gave us another quality veteran starter."

The Indians' offense garnered all the attention, and deservedly so. But the pitching staff ranked first in the AL in ERA. It might have lacked sizzle, but it certainly didn't lack any substance.

"I think it probably did deserve more attention," Hargrove said. "We were so prolific offensively, we probably would get overlooked. But we had one of the top bullpens in the game at that time. For a couple years, we did. Our starters were all solid guys, all solid No. 3s. Mark Wiley, our pitching coach, did a great job. Mark didn't get the credit as a pitching coach that he should have. He kept those guys focused. It's pretty amazing, truly."

It helped to have veteran catchers to guide the pitchers through each game. Tony Peña picked up much of the slack behind the plate while Sandy Alomar Jr. recovered from knee surgery. Peña had developed a particular rapport with Martínez, becoming El Presidente's personal catcher. The Indians duplicated their feat again in 1996, as they led the AL in ERA for a second consecutive season.

"It was a collective effort," Alomar said. "I have to say, Tony Peña really helped me a lot with that, how to mature as a catcher. Maturity as a catcher is not easy in the big leagues. You're going to get your poundings and you're going to have doubts, because when you're in development like I was earlier, we were getting pounded, because we were not throwing strikes. We were not growing up. Guys lacked confidence at times. You need somebody with experience who can help you and guide you through those losses. I got help from everybody. I had help from Joel Skinner in the past, Junior Ortiz. But at the right moment, I had Tony Peña. And Orel Hershiser and Dennis Martínez, those guys really helped me a lot with the transformation of who we were—not just me, but Charles Nagy and some other guys, too. Those guys were great for our team."

Said Wiley, "A lot was said about our offense, and rightfully so. But if you looked at the games, you would be surprised how many times we were tied or maybe a run down through six innings. That's why our bullpen, we had two bullpen guys who had a lot of wins. We put pressure on the other teams because we had a great lineup, but because our pitching held them so much, the pressure mounted on the other team."

Five Most Impressive Pitching Performances of the 1995 Regular Season

The Indians' pitchers contended they didn't mind that the club's offense hogged the spotlight. That's admirable, considering how effective the staff was on the mound. Indians starters logged eight or more innings in 20 of the team's 144 games, and the team went 18–2 in those contests. They led the American League with four complete-game shutouts. Not to mention, the bullpen was as proficient as any in baseball.

But who authored the most impressive single-game performances on the mound in 1995? Let's examine five that stand tall.

Orel Hershiser: June 5 against the Tigers at Jacobs Field

The stat line: Complete-game, six-hit shutout with no walks and 10 strikeouts, 107 pitches, 72 strikes

Hershiser allowed five harmless singles and a double as the Indians thumped the Tigers 8–0. Detroit's rookie outfielder Bobby Higginson went 3-for-3 against Hershiser; the rest of Sparky Anderson's lineup went 3-for-29. Hershiser was in the zone from the get-go, as he struck out the Tigers swinging—Chad Curtis, Lou Whitaker, and Travis Fryman—in order on 14 pitches in the first inning. Hershiser was no stranger to the late innings, as he logged at least six innings in 21 of his 26 starts, and at least seven innings in 15 of the 26. He only went the distance on this one occasion, though, a masterpiece against the Tigers.

Charles Nagy: September 13 against the Yankees at Jacobs Field

The stat line: Complete-game, three-hit shutout with two walks and five strikeouts, 115 pitches, 73 strikes

The names in the Yankees' lineup carried a lot of weight: Wade Boggs, Bernie Williams, Paul O'Neill, Darryl Strawberry, Mike Stanley, Don Mattingly. And Buck Showalter's bunch was jockeying for the American League's first-ever Wild Card berth, as the new playoff wrinkle had been introduced a year earlier, before the strike wiped out the postseason. The Yankees, Mariners, Rangers, and even the Royals were vying for a playoff spot—though the Mariners would ultimately storm back in the AL West race and catch the Angels for the division crown.

Still, by mid-September, every Yankees game was critical. The Indians had already secured their ticket to October. Their motivation stemmed from the pursuit of personal achievements and boosting the team's win total. The Yankees registered the only winning record by a visiting team at Jacobs Field in 1995 (4–2). They entered the series finale on a six-game winning streak. But Nagy, after twiddling his thumbs during a 77–minute rain delay, silenced New York's bats with a three-hit shutout.

Just how desperate were the Yankees? Showalter said after the loss, "We don't use playing the Indians in their ballpark as an excuse to lose a game. We have to win games." To be fair, it is no easy task to sweep a team that stands at 89–39, including 49–16 at home. The 5–0 defeat did temporarily knock the Yankees from pole position in the Wild Card race.

Chad Ogea: July 6 against the Mariners at Jacobs Field
The stat line: Complete game, one run allowed on three hits, no walks, three strikeouts

Even without Ken Griffey Jr. hitting third, the Mariners presented a competent, powerful lineup, one that regularly gave the Indians fits in 1995. Ogea had no trouble navigating Lou Piniella's batting order, though. Ogea made four appearances for the Indians in 1994, but the 1995 campaign was his rookie season, and he dazzled. He posted a 3.05 ERA over 106⅓ innings. His signature outing came against the Mariners, when he submitted a three-hitter and needed only 82 pitches to cruise through nine innings in an 8–1 win.

Ogea also delivered a few unforgettable relief appearances. On three occasions in 1995, he logged more than four innings out of the bullpen. On May 6, he spared the bullpen by throwing 4⅓ scoreless innings of relief in a 5–2 loss to the Twins. On June 4, he replaced an ineffective Jason Grimsley in the first inning and covered the next 6⅔ innings, while allowing only one run. That provided the Indians' offense with the opportunity to convert an 8–0 deficit into a 9–8 victory. On August 15, Nagy failed to escape the first inning, as he surrendered six runs to the Orioles. Ogea took over with two outs and he took it the distance. He pitched the final 7⅓ innings, throwing 94 pitches in relief, while limiting Baltimore to two runs.

Jose Mesa and Jim Poole: May 7 against the Twins at Jacobs Field

The stat line: 7⅓ scoreless innings, three hits, three walks, five strikeouts, 83 pitches, 50 strikes

Okay, so perhaps this is cheating, but Mesa and Poole deserve to share a bit of the spotlight for their efforts in the Indians' 17-inning marathon against the Twins on May 7. The Indians (well, namely Grimsley) coughed up an 8–3 advantage in the late innings and the teams took a 9–9 tie into extra innings. Mesa, Cleveland's seventh pitcher of the afternoon, recorded the final out of the 10th inning. He then proceeded to pitch a scoreless 11th, 12th, and 13th—his longest outing of the year. Poole then quieted Minnesota's bats for the next four innings, his longest outing since September 1991. The Twins turned to four different relievers over the same timeframe. Mesa and Poole helped to bide time for the Indians' offense, as Kenny Lofton's 17th-inning single—the club's 26th hit of the game—produced the Indians' first walk-off win of the season.

Dennis Martínez: June 13 against the Orioles at Jacobs Field

The stat line: Complete-game shutout, eight hits allowed, one walk, three strikeouts, 124 pitches, 83 strikes

Even at the age of 41, while wading through his 20th season in the major leagues, Martínez's right arm could handle a heavy workload. Ten days earlier, Martínez tossed a complete-game shutout against the Blue Jays. He scattered nine hits and he threw 113 pitches. Five days earlier, Martínez surrendered five runs (four earned) against the Brewers, though the Indians eked out an 8–7 victory. Martínez threw 114 pitches over six innings. On June 13, Martínez submitted another complete-game shutout, this time against the Orioles, who boasted a more-than-formidable middle of the order, with Rafael Palmeiro, Cal Ripken Jr., and Harold Baines all batting better than .300 at the time. But Martínez carved them up in the Indians' 11–0 victory. He moved to 6–0 on the season (he would start 9–0 before dropping four straight decisions) with a 124–pitch gem, his second-highest pitch count of the season.

6

"We Just Started Slapping Guys"

TO PAUL SHUEY, THE MOUND at Dodger Stadium might as well have been a coffin. When manager Jim Tracy summoned him from the bullpen, with Los Angeles clinging to a slim advantage, the pressure to protect that lead nearly suffocated the right-handed reliever.

"It was like, 'Ooh, you better shut it down,'" Shuey said.

Shuey had no margin for error. One slight slip-up and he would be forced to hand the ball to his manager, saunter toward the dugout, and avoid eye contact with his peeved peers who provided that lead in the first place. That is the tightrope most relievers must traverse. The role requires a short memory, an affinity for angst, and an involuntary numbness in the face of agony.

That never was the case in Cleveland, though, where Shuey pitched for nine seasons. He broke into the big leagues in 1994, two years after the Indians selected him with the second overall pick in the amateur draft. In '94 and '95, he dipped his toes in the water before he ultimately emerged as a familiar face in the late innings. During the 1995 postseason, he kept his arm in shape as a member of the Indians' reserve squad, a small group of players who remained one call away in case of an injury.

With the Indians, Shuey's goal was a bit different, and quite a bit more attainable. Preserve the lead or face the wrath of 24 hornets with their stingers poised to strike? Not exactly.

"It was like, 'Nah, just keep it close,'" Shuey said, "'because Manny is coming up. Or Thome is coming up. Or Albert is going to get the clutch hit.' I came up in '94. They had all of the studs' studs."

Shuey can remember retreating to the dugout after surrendering the lead one game, only to discover a collection of teammates who weren't the least bit concerned about the digits on the scoreboard. What did they say to comfort the reliever?

Don't worry about it. It's all right. Next inning, when you get back in there, you'll be up a run. Don't worry about it.

"And then when it happens," Kenny Lofton said, "he's like, 'Oh, shoot! Yeah!'

Just throw strikes. Don't be walking people. Make them earn it. And if they earn it, we've got you.

"That's what we had, man," Lofton said. "It was crazy. We didn't care who was on the mound, or which team. We didn't care. That's the attitude everyone had, that we were the best team, so we don't care."

So how would Lofton characterize that attitude? Is it cockiness? Is it merely confidence, or some degree of self-assurance? Whatever it was, it fueled the Indians in 1995.

"Some guys were a little over the top," Lofton said. "I always say, if you go out and you're going to go and be cocky, you have to go out there and put the numbers up. You have to perform. Once you do that, you can't say nothin'. Muhammad Ali said, 'I'm a bad man. I'm the greatest of all time.' All of a sudden, he knocks somebody on their butt. So there's nothing you can say. We walked the walk and we talked the talk. We talked the talk and we walked the walk."

Jason Giambi was a wide-eyed rookie infielder for the Oakland Athletics in 1995. His club went 0–7 against the Indians that year. The Indians were the measuring stick. Teams especially dreaded making the death march to Jacobs Field, the least accommodating venue in the league for an opponent—on the diamond, at least.

"If you could go into Cleveland and play well, you knew what kind of ball club you had," Giambi said, "because they were so good

---

Walk-Off No. 1

Game: Game 10, May 7

Opponent: Minnesota Twins

Final score: 10–9 (in 17 innings)

When Mike Hargrove shifted to the opposite end of the dugout, the stalemate finally ceased. Hargrove relocated for the 17th inning and, naturally, the Indians broke through. In the game's 396th minute, and on the game's 580th pitch, against the game's 17th pitcher and with the game's 132nd baseball, Kenny Lofton punched a base hit up the middle, through a drawn-in Twins defense. It stands as the longest game, time-wise, in franchise history, and it concluded with a rather tame celebration.

Lofton joked that he was so tired by that point—he collected four hits in 10 at-bats, stole two bases and roamed the center field grass for a few hours—that he ran straight to the clubhouse, showered, and headed home. This was not one of those patented home-plate parties with props and helmet pounding. This was about exhaling. The Indians hosted the Royals the next evening. The Twins had to hop on a flight, about three hours later than desired, and travel to Chicago, unable to celebrate a series victory while in the air.

---

and so stacked that if you could play with them, you had a good team."

The Indians amassed a 54–18 record at home, outscoring the opposition by 128 runs. That equates to a robust .750 winning percentage. According to real statistics that are not at all made up to drive home a point, you have a better chance at being struck by lightning, winning the Mega Millions, or being eaten by a shark than an opposing team had of winning multiple games in a series at Jacobs Field in 1995.

The Indians notched 12 walk-off wins (not to mention 27 victories in their last at-bat and 51 come-from-behind wins), so fans knew never to make a beeline for the exits before the ninth inning. The team went 13–0 in games that required extra innings.

The Indians made every opponent's flight out of Hopkins International Airport a miserable, spiritless journey to the next city. Those poor flight attendants. *No, we don't want any mini pretzels; we just had our asses handed to us.*

And the Indians took pride in delivering those sucker punches. They craved that feeling of leaving the opponent limp and lifeless. During a visit to the Indians' clubhouse in 2019, Carlos Baerga recalled that mindset when chatting with Francisco Lindor at his corner locker.

"You know what we used to have?" Baerga asked the All-Star shortstop. "We believed in ourselves so much that every time we stepped onto the field, we were going to crush people. If we were going to Kansas City or Milwaukee, we were going to win the series no matter what. We were going to beat you three games in a row. That was the mentality that we had in there."

Walk-Off No. 2

Game: Game 13, May 10
Opponent: Kansas City Royals
Final score: 3–2 (in 10 innings)

One aspect that often gets overlooked is that many of the Indians' late-game heroics were made possible by dazzling pitching performances. On a brisk, damp night at Jacobs Field in mid-May, Wayne Kirby supplied a pinch-hit, game-tying single in the ninth inning off Royals closer Jeff Montgomery. Ruben Amaro, who had pinch-run for Paul Sorrento following the first baseman's leadoff walk, scored the tying run. That prevented Charles Nagy from receiving a tough-luck loss after he limited Kansas City to two runs on four hits and no walks over eight innings. Montgomery, a three-time All-Star who racked up 304 saves in his career, faced the Indians four times in 1995. They scratched across at least one run against him in three of those encounters.

Carlos Baerga doubled to begin the bottom of the 10th. Three batters later, Manny Ramirez singled to center and Baerga slid under the tag of Royals catcher Pat Borders and into home plate umpire Mike Reilly. The throw from center fielder Tom Goodwin beat Baerga to the plate, but Borders set up in front of the plate to wait for the ball, so he had to twist his body to swipe Baerga with a tag, and when he completed the motion, the baseball squirted free from his glove and gave the Indians the green light to spill out of the dugout for an old-fashioned mobbing at home plate.

"I always hear now about, 'This team has had this many walk-offs, and this and that,'" pitching coach Mark Wiley said. "And I go, 'I don't know how anybody could have had more walk-offs than we did.' It was unbelievable."

Walk-Off No. 3

Game: Game 34, June 4
Opponent: Toronto Blue Jays
Final score: 9–8

Here is how Jason Grimsley's Sunday afternoon start unfolded:

Walk.

Walk.

Walk.

Single.

Single.

Sacrifice bunt. (An analytical angel just lost its wings.)

Three-run home run.

Walk.

For those scoring at home, that's seven runs on three hits and four walks in one-third of an inning, and he only recorded that lone out because the Blue Jays opted to have eventual Hall of Famer Roberto Alomar drop down a bunt in the middle of a fully formed and high-functioning conga line.

No matter. Once the top of the first inning subsided, the Indians' win expectancy sat at 8 percent. When Devon White tacked on a sacrifice fly against Chad Ogea in the third inning, the Indians' win expectancy sat at 3 percent. Oh, and they were facing David Cone, the reigning American League Cy Young Award winner. But rolling over just did not jibe with the mojo of a dugout stocked with confident sluggers.

"We wanted to do so well," Carlos Baerga said. "We never gave up, no matter if we were losing in the seventh, in the eighth; we always tried to come back. That showed the kind of character the team had in there, the attitude and the character."

The Indians closed to within 8–6 in the ninth, but they still needed a fortuitous bounce or two. Albert Belle's chopper took a wicked hop once it reached Alomar's territory in short right field, and it skipped away from the typically sure-handed second baseman, resulting in a single. Eddie Murray then slapped a single down the right-field line and Jim Thome hustled down the base path to beat out a potential game-ending double play. That scored Belle to shave the deficit to a single run.

Eight days earlier, with the Indians trailing the Blue Jays 3–0 in the ninth inning north of the border, Toronto reliever Darren Hall shattered Paul Sorrento's bat on an outside pitch. The result: Sorrento, the potential tying run, grounded into a game-ending, 6-4-3 double play.

On this afternoon, though, Hall left a pitch over the plate and Sorrento sent it soaring over the right-field fence for a walk-off, two-run home run. The Indians' win expectancy? One hundred percent.

"Our offense was really good that year," Sorrento said. "We were losing that game the whole game and to come back like that was definitely a highlight for that season, for sure. That may have been my only walk-off home run in my career, too. I think it was."

(Don't sell yourself short, Paul. You hit one on May 27, 1994, off Oakland's John Briscoe, for a 3–2 Indians win.)

On the TV broadcast, Rick Manning proclaimed, "The magic's back!"

If staking the reigning Cy Young Award winner to an eight-run lead was not safe against the Indians' lineup, what was?

"We found a way to create traffic on the bases," Sandy Alomar said. "We had so much power in the lineup, we could come back in any game really fast. So if you had a seven- or eight-run deficit early in the game, we could come back."

"When we played against Boston, when we played teams that were really good, we wanted to at least win two games out of three or three games out of four. Everybody talked about it. When the Indians came to town, they said, 'That team, the cockiness that they play with, we want to beat those guys,'" Baerga said.

Walk-Off No. 4

Game: Game 37, June 7

Opponent: Detroit Tigers

Final score: 3–2 (in 10 innings)

Twenty-four years after this game, Jim Thome had his memory tested at an All-Star Week function in Cleveland. During a Thome Trivia segment, the Hall of Fame slugger had to name the poor sap who surrendered Thome's first career walk-off home run. It was Brian Maxcy's seventh career major league appearance, and he had yet to yield his first run. David Wells logged nine sterling innings and Maxcy took over in the 10th. He started Thome with three consecutive sinkers that plunged out of the strike zone, low and inside. Thome peered into the dugout, checking to see if he would be granted the green light.

He got it. Ballgame.

Thome launched the 3–0 offering over the Office Max sign plastered onto the right-field wall. He tossed away his bat; he would not be needing that any longer. Once he touched home plate, he crouched down and guarded his helmet from his teammates' slap-happy hands.

The next night, Thome delivered another game-winning homer in the top of the ninth in Milwaukee.

"If you were down by anything less than seven going into the ninth, it was just a question of who was going to be the hero," said Jim Folk, "and you were trying to work your way through the lineup to figure it out."

Walk-Off No. 5

Game: Game 48, June 19
Opponent: Boston Red Sox
Final score: 4–3 (in 10 innings)

Even the most proficient data analyst in the world would struggle to pinpoint a set of arbitrary dates that reveals a Manny Ramirez slump during the 1995 season. Perhaps the best anyone could do is note his early-June struggles, as he started the month in an 8-for-42 funk. That's a miniature sample size, of course, and he still entered the Indians' tilt against the Red Sox on June 19 with a .340/.441/.660 slash line for the season, an absurd level of output for a kid who had turned 23 just three weeks earlier.

Ramirez wasn't thrilled with his June stretch, though, so he visited Mike Hargrove in the manager's office, across the hall from the home clubhouse, for the first time. He closed the door behind him, grabbed a bat, and started to attempt to dissect what he thought was ailing him at the plate. Hargrove agreed with Ramirez's self-diagnosis, and they devoted a half-hour to identifying a remedy.

The Indians erased a 3–0 deficit against Boston later that night. Red Sox reliever Ken Ryan caught Ramirez looking in the eighth, with the go-ahead run standing in scoring position. Ryan also struck out Wayne Kirby and Kenny Lofton to halt the Indians' threat. Ramirez and Ryan clashed again to start the bottom of the 10th. Ramirez thought he was pulling off when he swung, but he assured pitcher Dennis Martínez that he would not fail if he faced Ryan a second time. He just needed to remain in his stance and try to punish the ball to the opposite field.

And that is precisely what he did. On the eighth pitch of their encounter, Ramirez launched Ryan's 3–2 offering beyond the fence in right-center for the Indians' fifth walk-off win of the season.

"It was crazy to me the way we could come back," Wiley said. "If we were three runs down, like Buddy [Bell] said, it was like, 'Okay, we've got this.' It just happened."

The Indians were certainly cocky. And they knew they were cocky.

"We talked the talk," Lofton said. "We talked it, and we walked it. That's what made it so fun. It was like, 'Whoa.' A lot of people can talk it and not do it. But we had our chest high, like, 'We know who we are as individuals and nobody is going to take that away.'

"We worked *hard*. I think that's what people didn't see on the inside of it—we worked hard in spring training. We worked hard in the cages. We worked hard before the game, all of the preparation. We put the work in. And we knew it paid off *because* of the work we put in."

It is not as though the Indians formed that reputation overnight. First, they had to prove to themselves that they could win games. That started in 1994, before the players' strike. A 10-game winning streak in mid-June pushed the club into first place in the American

Walk-Off No. 6

Game: Game 71, July 16
Opponent: Oakland Athletics
Final score: 5–4 (in 12 innings)

If there was one word that could describe the Indians' 1995 regular season, Dennis Eckersley muttered it as dinner time approached on a Sunday evening in mid-July.

The Indians selected Eckersley—a 2004 Baseball Hall of Fame inductee—in the third round of the 1972 amateur draft, and he spent his first three big-league seasons with the franchise. In 1977, Eckersley made his first All-Star team, but the Indians traded him to Boston, where he blossomed into a Cy Young contender. In his first season with the Red Sox, he won 20 games, chewed up 268 innings, and finished fourth in the balloting for the coveted award.

When he joined the Athletics in 1987, Eckersley transitioned to the back end of the bullpen under manager Tony La Russa, who reinvented the way teams deployed relievers. From 1987 to '92, Eckersley registered a 2.18 ERA, with more than a strikeout per inning and an average of nearly 40 saves per season. In 1992, he racked up 51 saves, made the All-Star team for the third consecutive year, and captured both the AL Cy Young Award and the AL MVP Award.

By 1995, Eckersley had reached the age of 40 and crossed the 3,000-inning plateau. He no longer threatened to post a sub-1.00 ERA and instead hung around the 4.00 mark. He still owned the closer's role in Oakland, and on July 16, 1995, he entered the game in the bottom of the 12th inning, with the Athletics holding a 4–3 lead. Kenny Lofton stood on second base with two outs as Manny Ramirez approached the plate.

On the seventh pitch of the battle, Ramirez launched Eckersley's 2–2 fastball halfway up the bleachers in left field. The two-run homer secured the four-game sweep for the Indians, their first in franchise history against the Athletics. It was Ramirez's third consecutive game with a home run. Eckersley turned and watched the baseball sail into the stands, too. As he walked off the mound toward Oakland's dugout, Eckersley flashed a sheepish grin, impressed with Ramirez's mix of might and timeliness. There was no sign of frustration or disappointment, just astonishment. He simply mouthed the word, "Wow"—three letters befitting another Tribe walk-off win during a summer filled with them.

"We beat every top closer in the game," Wiley said. "We walked off every top closer in the game. Eckersley. Montgomery. You name it. We walked every one of them off, and some guys multiple times in the season."

Walk-Off No. 7

Game: Game 73, July 18
Opponent: California Angels
Final score: 7–5

The California Angels rattled off a 22–6 stretch from early July to early August, in which they outscored their opponents by 107 runs. The monthlong run provided them with an 11-game cushion in the AL West, an insurmountable deficit for the Mariners and Rangers. Or so everyone thought. Smack dab in the middle of the Angels' surge, Marcel Lachemann's club visited Cleveland for a quick, two-game trip. The Angels claimed the first contest 8–3 behind 6⅔ strong innings from Brian Anderson, a northeast Ohio native who would join the Indians via trade the following February.

The Angels gripped a ninth-inning lead in the second game, too, so in came Lee Smith, searching for his major league–record (at the time) 457th career save. Smith held the opposition scoreless in his first 20 appearances of the season. He finally surrendered his first run in late June. With the Angels on top 5–3, Smith served up singles to Wayne Kirby and Omar Vizquel around a Jim Thome strikeout. Kirby's single caromed off the bag at first base and out of J.T. Snow's reach. Vizquel smacked a line drive off the tip of shortstop Gary Disarcina's glove. Smith walked Carlos Baerga to load the bases. Baerga tossed his bat and turned toward Albert Belle to pump him up. As Belle stepped into the batter's box, the sellout crowd started to chant his first name.

On a 1–2 count, Smith hung a breaking ball over the outside part of the plate. Belle stretched his arms and broadcast his supreme strength, as he deposited the baseball over the center-field fence, into a cluster of picnic tables in the outfield pavilion.

Belle's 16th home run of the season—Smith said afterward that Belle "hit it in the pork and beans"—also marked the first walk-off grand slam in ballpark history. For the second time in a span of three days, the Indians tagged a future Hall of Fame pitcher with a walk-off blast.

The Angels rebounded from the shocking defeat and won 15 of their next 17 games, but they sure could have used that near-victory that slipped away. On the morning of August 17, they held a 10.5-game edge in the AL West, but thanks to a 6–24 stretch, that lead evaporated and forced them into a one-game playoff against the Mariners, with a ticket to the postseason on the line. Mariners ace Randy Johnson tossed a complete-game gem with 12 strikeouts to deliver the final blow in a 9–1 Seattle triumph. So, in an indirect way, Belle's blast prevented the Angels from qualifying for the playoffs.

The following season, during a game in Anaheim, the Indians broke a 1–1 tie in the ninth inning with three solo home runs in a span of five batters. Belle, Alomar, and Thome all went deep against Troy Percival, the Angels' new, young, hard-throwing All-Star closer. Four months later at Jacobs Field, the Indians scored four runs in the ninth, capped by a Manny Ramirez walk-off three-run blast, to sink Percival and the Angels 7–5.

"This guy was one of the best closers in all of baseball," Wiley said. "Marcel Lachemann and I are good friends and I used to kid him and say, 'Marcel, why didn't he throw his curveball more? He had a plus curveball.' And he goes, 'He would just give in to the macho thing, Mark. He would give in to the macho thing and say, 'I can throw my fastball by anybody.' But our guys were as good of a fastball-hitting team as there has ever been."

League Central. When the season was canceled, the Indians trailed the White Sox by one game, but they knew they were onto something.

"Everything was working," Mark Shapiro said. "We were getting to be a good team."

The Indians started that season 14–17, including their thrilling Opening Day victory in 11 innings against the Mariners to christen Jacobs Field, but they racked up a 52–30 record after that point, with the lineup enjoying a summer surge.

"That's why we went out and added Dennis [Martínez] and Orel [Hershiser] and Eddie [Murray] into the mix," assistant general manager Dan O'Dowd said. "We knew that was when we needed to turn the corner."

Martínez, Murray, and catcher Tony Peña served as the veteran leaders on a relatively young squad in 1994. Martínez and Murray signed free-agent pacts with the Indians on the same December day in 1993. Dave Winfield joined the Indians in a deal with the Twins after the strike began in 1994. Originally, the agreement mandated that the Indians ship the Twins a player to be named later. The clubs scrapped that clause when the players' strike commenced, and instead, the Indians' brass picked up the tab at a dinner between the organizations' front office executives. Winfield re-signed with the Indians for the 1995 season, joining fellow veteran free-agent addition Orel Hershiser.

"He was kind of playing through an injury, but he's still Dave Winfield," Paul Sorrento said. "He was off of our bench. We had Wayne Kirby coming off our bench. Both of those guys would have been playing for a lot of teams."

So, the 1995 Indians had a balanced blend of experienced veterans and confident, rising stars. That's a healthy combination.

"It was a crazy ride, but that's the way that team went," Hargrove said. "Those guys never felt like there was a game they were out of, no matter what the circumstances were. They felt there was going to be something that would happen in the last few innings. The thing is, when we did get a break, we capitalized on it. I remember when we played the Orioles in '97 in the playoffs and somebody asked me the

---

Walk-Off No. 8

Game: Game 104, August 19
Opponent: Milwaukee Brewers
Final score: 4–3

On July 2, just two days after he joined the 3,000-hit club, Eddie Murray sustained two broken ribs on his left side during a slide into home plate. Murray delivered an RBI double during a four-run third inning at the Metrodome. Jim Thome singled him home, but Twins catcher Matt Walbeck supplied a hard tag, and during the collision at the plate, Murray suffered an injury that would keep him sidelined for a month. He tried to bat in the fifth but exited the game after taking the first pitch. Herbert Perry finished the at-bat.

Even when he returned from the injured list, Murray still felt soreness when he batted right-handed. On August 19, he went hitless in his first three trips to the plate, all against southpaw Scott Karl. Then the Brewers summoned righty reliever Bill Wegman to preserve the 3–3 tie. Wegman mowed down the Indians in order in the eighth, but Murray would get to bat left-handed to start the ninth. The prescient Tony Peña had told Murray before the game that he was due for a game-winning home run. And Murray promptly launched Wegman's 2–0 pitch into the right-field seats for the Tribe's eighth walk-off of the season.

---

difference between the two teams and that was the year the Orioles were in first from wire to wire. And I said, 'The difference is, when we get breaks, we take advantage of it. Baltimore hasn't.' That's how the '95 team was, too."

Wiley had worked for the organization since the late '80s. He had survived the 100-loss seasons, the chilly, eerily quiet nights on

---

Walk-Off No. 9

Game: Game 109, August 25
Opponent: Detroit Tigers
Final score: 6–5 (in 11 innings)

Albert Belle belted a couple of home runs to celebrate his 29th birthday, but the Indians' bullpen squandered a pair of late-inning leads. Jose Mesa surrendered a solo, opposite-field home run to Chad Curtis with two outs in the ninth to account for the closer's first blown save of the season. It snapped his record streak of 37 consecutive save conversions. His ERA skyrocketed to 1.25. The horror!

Curtis' homer forced the game into extra innings and allowed Sandy Alomar Jr. to deliver a magical memory. A kid in attendance had recently lost his father in a car crash. The kid told Alomar he was his favorite player and that he was bound to hit a home run that night. Alomar had not hit a home run in a month. In fact, over the previous month, he had posted a .239 batting average and a .530 OPS. His average had tumbled to .298 from .386.

Maybe he was due. Maybe a higher power intervened and made him a hero that night. Maybe it was simply perfect timing and fortune. Alomar golfed Felipe Lira's 1–1 offering onto the home run porch in left field. He handed the kid his bat and later signed it for him in the clubhouse.

"He was built for the special moments," Carlos Baerga said.

---

the lakefront. And he marveled at the strides the club made in a couple quick years. Before games, he would peer at the opposing dugout and run through each positional matchup in his head. For a long time, the routine did nothing but highlight the franchise's talent void.

Walk-Off No. 10

Game: Game 114, August 30
Opponent: Toronto Blue Jays
Final score: 4–3 (in 14 innings)

The Indians and Blue Jays traded sacrifice flies in the 14th inning, but as the game approached the five-hour mark, Albert Belle approached the plate, aiming to send everyone home. Belle thought Tony Castillo would pitch around him. Light-hitting Wayne Kirby was on deck. There were two outs. There was not much of a reason to challenge Belle, who had produced an .833 slugging percentage and a 1.301 OPS in August. Spoiler alert: he would somehow enhance those numbers over the final two days of the month.

Belle decided he would hack away at anything near the strike zone...or anything near his zip code. He fouled off a pitch that sailed high and outside, about level with his face. A few pitches later, Castillo tossed another pitch high and outside, about even with Belle's shoulders, and Belle somehow powered it over the center-field wall.

Trailing in the 14th inning? No big deal. This method of waiting until the last possible moment to pull out a victory had become routine.

"There wasn't any difference from a walk-off win to a win," Kenny Lofton said. "We felt like a win is a win is a win. It just happened to be a walk-off."

"I'd look over to the other dugout," Wiley said, "and I would go, 'Oh, my God.' There would be, like, seven guys better than our guys starting. And I would go, 'This is going to be tough.'"

That changed, though. In 1995, he would sort through the opposing roster and smile. Was their left fielder more powerful than Albert Belle? Not a chance. Was the center fielder more explosive than Kenny Lofton? Of course not. Was their shortstop as gifted with the glove as Omar Vizquel? No way. Did they have .300 hitters at second base, third base, and right field? In their dreams.

"Once we got really good," Wiley said, "I told the guys, 'Now, I look over and it's the exact opposite. Every one of our position players is better, except for a couple guys on the other team.' That alone was big, and then the fact that we had such a consistent and durable pitching staff, that played into it."

The fan base certainly bought into the team's arrival. On June 7, 1995, Thome treated a crowd of 36,363 to a walk-off home run in the 10th inning against the Tigers, a powerful cap to a pitcher's duel between David Wells and Charles Nagy. The Indians then traveled to Milwaukee for a four-game series. They returned to Cleveland with a 30–11 record and a comfortable lead in the division standings. And they returned for a Monday night battle against Baltimore at Jacobs Field, where a crowd of 41,845 filled the ballpark to capacity. Thus, the famed sellout streak was born, the first of 455 consecutive games the Indians played at Jacobs Field in which no green seat and no spot on a metal bench in the bleachers went unoccupied. John Hart compared the atmosphere to a college football setting, a stadium full of engaged fans living and dying with every pitch.

"This place was rocking all the time," Giambi said. "It was so hard to take the crowd out of it here. No matter how many runs you put up, as soon as they got one runner on, the crowd started getting back

Walk-Off No. 11

Game: Game 115, August 31
Opponent: Toronto Blue Jays
Final score: 6–4 (in 10 innings)

Albert Belle watched rookie Jimmy Rogers warm up before the 10th inning. He noticed a fastball, a curveball, and a slider in his repertoire. When Belle stepped into the batter's box, with Jim Thome on first base and one out, Rogers greeted him with a curveball that spun out of the strike zone. Rogers then shifted to his slider, which Belle fouled back. So that left the fastball. And Rogers did not place it far enough up and in, if that ideal location even exists when facing a powerful free-swinger like Belle. The Indians' clean-up hitter yanked the fastball to the home run porch for a decisive, two-run shot, his second walk-off homer in as many nights.

It had only been two months since a Tribe player (Thome) hit a game-winning home run in the ninth inning or later in back-to-back games. But Belle's feat would be the last time that occurred until Carlos Santana did so in August 2019.

The Indians wrapped up their season series against the Blue Jays with a 10–3 record, including three walk-off wins, their most versus any opponent.

"There were not too many downs. There were a lot of ups," Charles Nagy said. "You were never out of any games. Through that whole time of winning in Cleveland, the other teams hated coming to Jacobs Field. They just couldn't wait to get out of there. Talking to them before the series, before games, after games, they were just glad when they knew they could leave Jacobs Field, because they knew they were in for a long three or four days being there. That just fueled everything on our side, knowing that, 'Hey, we're never out of any of these games and these guys are scared.'"

into it. It was such a home-field advantage. That's what I remember as a player coming here. It was unbelievable."

The Indians became the first team in the league to sell every ticket to every game for an entire season, a feat they accomplished for five straight years (1996 to 2000). They eclipsed the Rockies' record streak by 252 games, more than three seasons' worth. The Red Sox eventually topped the sellout record in 2008.

"We beat the Yankees in in-park attendance for several years in the '90s," said Jim Folk, the Indians' vice president of ballpark operations. "In Cleveland, for crying out loud. Who would have thought that?"

On June 20, 1995, the 1,000,000[th] fan passed through the turnstiles, the fastest the Indians had ever reached that mark. They finished the season with 2.84 million fans, a franchise record at that point, even though they hosted only 72 games because of the strike. The only other time the team came close to matching that attendance total was in 1948, when the World Series winners attracted 2.62 million to the lakefront. In the 30 seasons from 1956 to '85, the Indians only topped 1 million fans on five occasions.

From the time Jacobs Field opened its doors in 1994 until the end of the streak in 2001, the Indians sold out 95 percent of their regular season games. They attracted more than 19 million fans to the ballpark during the streak. The Indians fell one game short of qualifying for the postseason in 2000, and ticket sales suffered entering the next season. Fans packed the venue on Opening Day, but only 32,763 attended the second game of the season, about three-fourths of the stadium's capacity. It marked the club's first non-sellout in 2,122 days.

From 1956 to 1985, the Indians drew 24,549,689 fans.

From 1995 to 2002, the Indians drew 25,750,165 fans.

"It was the place to go," Giambi said. "It was unbelievable. They were selling out every game. Some of the best players in the game were playing there. The fans were coming out in droves, the Flats, that city was bumping. It was fun to play there."

Well, the home team and its fans were the ones having the most fun, with one memorable finish after another.

"I expected the moments," Shuey said. "It wasn't, 'Man, I wonder.' It was, 'Who? Is it going to be Manny? Is it going to be Thome? Is it going to be Albert?'"

The walk-off celebrations started in 1994 with soft, controlled taps of the helmet when the players congregated at home plate. With each

---

Walk-Off No. 12

Game: Game 143, September 30
Opponent: Kansas City Royals
Final score: 3–2 (in 10 innings)

The Indians actually went a month without recording a single walk-off win. During that stretch, though, they clinched the division title, Albert Belle made a late charge at joining the 50-homer club, and the team flirted with the idea of a 100-win season.

They saved their final walk-off win for the penultimate game of the regular season. The Royals finished second in the American League Central standings, a mere 30 games behind the Indians. Cleveland swept the final series of the season to create the final separation.

This time, it was a Baerga single to center that scored rookie Jeromy Burnitz with one out in the bottom of the 10th.

The final walk-off leaderboard:

3: Belle, Ramirez

1: Alomar, Baerga, Lofton, Murray, Sorrento, Thome

"You were not wondering *if,*" Shuey said. "It was a race to say, 'It's going to be me.'"

---

win, the taps grew more intense. Over time, the helmet-knocking evolved into helmet-pounding. It reached a point in which hitters joked that they dreaded delivering a walk-off home run because it usually resulted in a headache the next day. Lofton quipped that he would sprint away from the pack and make his teammates, none of which possessed his level of foot speed, chase him around the ballpark.

"We just started slapping guys," Sandy Alomar Jr. said. "One time, I hit Thome so hard he felt like he had whiplash. It was getting to the point that guys were running to home plate and trying to touch home plate and then run away. You had Julian Tavarez and Jim Thome hitting guys, and Manny Ramirez. It was getting dangerous."

Especially since it happened so frequently.

Bell suggested that the Indians actually fared better at the plate when they faced a late-game deficit, as if they sometimes needed an extra push. Wiley surmised, "[That's when] they would lock in and they would focus.

"If we were down in the ninth inning," Wiley said, "[Buddy] would be like, 'Mark, we're three runs down. We get a guy on, we've got this.' It was the ninth inning! Most teams down three runs in the ninth inning, you're not going to win the game. And then we would hit a grand slam or a three-run home run and walk them off and Buddy and I would just look at each other and have our mouths wide open and our eyes wide open, looking at each other like, 'Wow.' It happened all the time."

Win No. 100

The Indians could have coasted into the postseason, ensuring their players were well-rested and safe from any nicks and bruises. Then again, imagine having to tell Albert Belle he would be spending his evening on the bench instead of at the plate, souring the self-esteem of every opposing pitcher. The Indians' position players wanted to keep playing. They wanted to keep winning. They clinched the American League Central on September 8. They had a little more than three weeks to catch their breath and assemble their playoff rotation.

So on the final day of the regular season, the Indians standing one win shy of 100 for the season, Mike Hargrove constructed his lineup as he would for any other meaningful game: Kenny Lofton leading off, followed by Omar Vizquel and Carlos Baerga, Belle in the cleanup spot, backed by Eddie Murray, Jim Thome, and Manny Ramirez, with Paul Sorrento and Sandy Alomar Jr. rounding out the starting nine.

The Indians entered the final day of the regular season with a 13–7 record since their clinching game. They had won four straight contests, and a Sunday afternoon victory would seal a three-game sweep of the second-place Royals. Now, Kansas City earned the distinction of AL Central runners-up only because *someone* had to technically finish second. The Royals wound up an MLB-record 30 games behind the Indians in the standings. The Indians went 11–1 against Kansas City in 1995, outscoring the Royals by a 76–28 margin.

The Indians wanted to end the regular season on a high note. It was their final chance to enhance their stat lines, one last opportunity to send the rest of the league a message about what it might encounter in October.

So Lofton started the bottom of the first with a single to center. And he stole second. And he stole third. Vizquel walked and

Baerga singled to score Lofton. Belle walked to load the bases and the parade started in earnest. Murray, Thome, and Ramirez each supplied an RBI single. Sorrento walked. That's eight batters and zero outs, for those keeping track. Poor Tom Gordon, Kansas City's sacrificial lamb on that sunny, 76-degree day. Gordon finally recorded a couple of outs, but Vizquel slapped an RBI single to left for the Indians' sixth run of the opening frame.

Gordon's day worsened in the second. Belle, Murray, and Thome all singled to start the inning. When Ramirez walked, Royals manager Bob Boone placed a call to his bullpen. The Indians totaled five more runs in the second. Lofton and Vizquel each batted three times in the first two innings. The Indians could have been on cruise control a couple days from their first playoff game in 41 years. Instead, they pounded the accelerator.

Hargrove didn't waste much time in turning to his bench. Alvaro Espinoza pinch-ran for Baerga in the first inning. Brian Giles ran for Murray in the second. Billy Ripken replaced Vizquel in the field before the third, with the Royals facing an early, Denali-sized task. Jeromy Burnitz and Ruben Amaro entered on defense for Lofton and Belle in the sixth, and Wayne Kirby and Dave Winfield pinch-hit for Ramirez and Sorrento in the seventh. Herbert Perry and Jesse Levis joined the fray in the late innings. In all, the Indians used 18 position players and four pitchers. Every player in the starting lineup exited the game early except for Thome.

Another six-run inning pushed the Indians' advantage to 17–4 in the fifth. Ripken and Sorrento smacked home runs, Giles contributed an RBI single and Lofton recorded an RBI triple, his league-leading (and career-high) 13th three-bagger of the season. The Indians totaled 17 runs on 19 hits and five walks. Somehow, the game only required two hours and 52 minutes to play, even though the Royals needed 172 pitches to record 24 outs.

It was the most fitting way to wrap up perhaps the most memorable regular season in team history. The Indians' 17 runs were a season high, their most in any game since May 4, 1991, when they bludgeoned the Athletics in Oakland 20–6. It marked their eighth game in which they won by at least 10 runs. And it gave the Indians the second 100-win season in franchise lore, despite the fact that they played a 144-game schedule. Their winning percentage of .694 put them on pace to achieve a 113–49 record over a typical 162-game schedule. That win total would have placed them second in major league history at the time, behind only the 1906 Chicago Cubs, who went 116–36. The 1998 Yankees (114–48) and 2001 Mariners (116–46) later joined the elite winners list.

The Indians finished with a similar record and run differential in each month in 1995.

May: 19–7 (+47 run differential)

June: 20–8 (+41)

July: 18–9 (+38)

August: 21–9 (+43)

September: 19–9 (+50)

"I have to believe if we played a 162-game season that year and played 18 more games," said Wiley, "that, as good as we were, we would have won 112, 114 games maybe. You don't know, but we lost four games in a row one time. That was to the White Sox. They were [17] games out or something, and they swept us, three in a row. They got all excited. I know there was concern with our front office and stuff. We [continued on] and we swept another team."

7

Drum Solos and Punchlines

FOLLOWING THE STRIKE-SHORTENED 1994 season, the Indians' marketing department hatched the idea for the Silver & Gold Affair. The event, held at the opening of Rock Bottom Brewery in the Flats, would honor Carlos Baerga, the Silver Slugger Award–winning second baseman, and Omar Vizquel, the Gold Glove Award–winning shortstop.

In 103 games that season, Baerga batted .314 with 19 home runs, 32 doubles, and an .858 OPS. Vizquel had an inauspicious introduction to his new teammates that year. He had already developed a reputation as a skilled fielder, as he earned his first Gold Glove Award with the Mariners in 1993. But on April 16, 1994, his ninth game as a member of the Indians, he committed three errors: a booted grounder and an errant throw on back-to-back plays in the third inning, and a misplayed pop fly with the bases loaded and the score tied in the eighth. Vizquel can recall a fan shouting from the stands, "Send this guy back to Seattle!"

"The first thing we said was, 'Who is this guy?'" Kenny Lofton remembered.

Vizquel then strung together 52 consecutive games without a miscue. He ended the season with six errors in all, and he captured his second straight Gold Glove Award, a streak that would ultimately reach nine years in a row.

So at the event, the middle-infield tandem posed with their awards. Fans could pay for a ticket to the event, plus an autographed photo of the duo. Baerga signed each photo with a silver pen; Vizquel signed each with a gold pen.

As the waitstaff tended to tables and the cooks tested out the new kitchen equipment, Vizquel noticed a band setting up to perform in the restaurant. Vizquel joined them on the drums. Baerga started to dance.

"Everybody in the place is like, 'Holy shit, this is the greatest'" said Bob DiBiasio, the Indians' vice president of public affairs. "That was the first time we were like, 'This dude is a renaissance man. He doesn't *just* have a canary yellow Porsche and dress different, but he does have these talents.'"

By 1995, the Indians had assembled a locker room full of outgoing personalities. It was quite the cocktail of characteristics. There was the intensity and fiery disposition of Albert Belle. There was the youthful exuberance of Julian Tavarez, Manny Ramirez, and Jim Thome. There was the flamboyance of Kenny Lofton. There were the even-keeled, calming presences of Eddie Murray, Orel Hershiser, Alvaro Espinoza, and Wayne Kirby.

"You know how you always have to have some light-hearted guys?" said pitching coach Mark Wiley. "We had Alvaro Espinoza and Wayne Kirby. They made humor in the dugout. They made it seem like we never had any pressure on us. They were cheerleaders. And then they did their job. Jim Thome was our third baseman. When we got a lead in the ninth inning, they usually put Alvaro in at third and took Jimmy out for defense. Kirby, he would take an outfield place if a guy got hurt or needed to come out for whatever reason. He would play one of the outfield spots, and I can't tell you how many times those guys made plays to save the game that maybe the other guy who was in there couldn't have made. It was perfect. They added some humor. They were really professional at what they did. They could get on players in the locker room, even though they weren't regular players, if they saw somebody was getting a big head or being too moody. We had a really good mix of guys and everybody got along really well."

And there was the boundless energy supplied by Vizquel and Baerga. They played percussion. They sang. They danced. They performed at comedy clubs. For Vizquel, those customs lasted throughout the '90s, but they really started in 1995.

"When there was a concert or they had a band, we used to go and watch it," Baerga said. "When Omar did stand-up comedy, we used to go there. We always looked for places to rest our minds from the field and take it outside."

Was Vizquel's comedic routine any good?

"Yeah! It's crazy, man," Baerga said. "Everything he does in life, he's done well. He's a joker. He makes people smile. He brings a story about everything."

Vizquel does not quite remember it going so smoothly. He said some audience members gave him a hard time, even yelling, "Don't ever quit your day job! You suck!" But Vizquel engaged in a lighthearted back-and-forth with his hecklers, which resulted in plenty of laughter.

"The kind of personality that the whole team had, everybody stuck out in different ways," Vizquel said. "When you say 'Omar', all the bright colors and the way that we used to talk and all that. I still have friends who, when they call me, they try to imitate my accent on the phone. That's just something that sticks out for everybody."

Other Cleveland Characters Who Could Have Fit in the '95 Clubhouse

Imagine, in one corner of the Indians' clubhouse, Carlos Santana dancing to blaring salsa music with Omar Vizquel and Carlos Baerga, while Francisco Lindor shouts ear-rattling, off-key lyrics from his locker. The '95 team was dripping with personality, and there have been plenty of colorful characters to take up residency in the home clubhouse at Progressive Field in the years following that 100-win season. Who would have fit in well among the chaos in 1995?

When Santana returned to the Indians for the 2019 season, it was like he never left, even though he spent a tumultuous 2018 campaign with the Phillies. Early in spring training, Santana grabbed the hand of hitting coach Ty Van Burkleo and started dancing behind the cage during on-field batting practice.

Here's a priceless moment we'll never witness: Jose Ramirez challenging Albert Belle to a round of Mario Kart. Ramirez's mentor during the 2016 season, Juan Uribe, would have complemented the group in fine fashion, too. One afternoon in Minneapolis that year, Ramirez and Santana equipped Uribe with a pair of bright pink water wings in the clubhouse. A wad of Kahlua-soaked tobacco often tucked in his cheek, Uribe, nicknamed "El Pavo," or "the turkey," seemed to go along with any of their shenanigans.

Speaking of shenanigans, Corey Kluber and Carlos Carrasco have proven quite skilled at pulling off pranks, especially in the stoic Kluber's stealthy style. Trot Nixon's postgame pie-to-the-face routine could have worked in 1995. Would Belle or Eddie

Murray have simply laughed off a face full of lemon meringue after notching a walk-off home run? Nick Swisher's unshakable enthusiasm would have added an interesting element. The brash bluntness of Chris Perez and Trevor Bauer would have worked for a team that had no problem voicing how it planned to dismantle its opponent before doing so. Or, picture a postseason-clinching celebration in which players are dashing across the clubhouse, dumping beer on their teammates and coaches. And then there's Joe Charboneau, in the middle of the chaos, opening beer bottles with his eye socket. Yeah, Super Joe would have meshed with that group.

Would Nyjer Morgan have meshed well with the '95 Indians? What about his alter ego, Tony Plush? Now that would be a sight to see. Manny Ramirez once saw a report on TV about O.J. Simpson and the white Bronco chase and thought it was about his teammate, Chad Ogea. Now imagine someone trying to explain to Ramirez that Morgan had a second identity named Tony Plush.

There is one recent member of the Indians who probably fits this prompt better than anyone: Yasiel Puig, who straddled the line between confident and arrogant. When Puig advanced on the bases during a game against the Twins in August 2019, he waved to Minnesota's outfielders, his way of telling them goodbye and that they had no chance of throwing him out. He twirls his bat like it's a baton, sometimes squats down to the dirt before a pitch, boasts an intimidating frame and often shouts across the clubhouse and has his teammates in stitches after wins. He also dyed his mohawk bright red upon his trade to Cleveland. Yeah, Puig would fit in quite well with the '95 group.

Throughout the summer of 1999, Paul Sidoti's trio played at Jimmy's in the Flats, on the banks of the Cuyahoga River in downtown Cleveland. The bar had a garage door that opened up to the sidewalk, so passersby could listen in, or even poke the drummer's back. On a Sunday at the end of August, the night before the Indians commenced a four-game set with the California Angels, manager Terry Collins and pitcher Chuck Finley—who would sign a free-agent contract with Cleveland four months later—walked into the bar. Sidoti, an avid baseball fan, immediately recognized them.

The band played the customary '80s hits: some Van Halen, The Outfield, Rick Springfield. Bryan Adams' "Summer of '69" was one of Sidoti's go-to tunes. Finley and Collins listened for about an hour. On their way out, Finley left a tip and told Sidoti, "You guys were great. You played all the songs I grew up on."

Two nights later, Sidoti returned to the bar. A group of local musicians gathered at Jimmy's on Tuesdays to watch a particular band. As the clocked ticked toward closing time, they all joined the band on stage. The Indians had defeated the Angels 14–12 earlier that evening, with Finley limiting the Tribe to one earned run over seven innings before the teams' bullpens set the world ablaze. The Indians erased a 12–4 deficit with a 10-run eighth, capped by a Richie Sexson three-run homer. (Those 1999 Indians were every bit the offensive juggernaut as the '95 club, as they became the first team in nearly a half-century to score 1,000 runs.) After Sexson's blast, Angels closer Troy Percival plunked David Justice, who charged the mound and sparked a benches-clearing brawl.

Finley entered the bar later that night with Indians southpaw (and former Angels hurler) Mark Langston. Finley pointed out Sidoti and said to Langston, "Mark, this is the guy I was telling you about, the guitar player."

Langston brought his own guitar on road trips, and he and Sexson would jam out in their hotel rooms before and after they headed to the ballpark. When Langston broke into the big leagues with the Mariners in the mid-80s, a member of Magic Bus, a Seattle-based band, taught him how to play the instrument.

"I would go, 'Hey, how do you play 'Hold on Loosely,' by .38 Special?'" Langston said. "Instead of having any teaching, he would just show me songs." Magic Bus wound up serving as the house band for the first installment of Tribe Jam, a rock concert at Nautica Pavilion, on the banks of the Cuyahoga River, that featured Indians players on the microphone and various instruments. The team put on a concert for three consecutive summers.

Sidoti instantly connected with the pitchers. He worked for KISS on the band's Psycho Circus tour over the previous year. Finley occasionally played golf with KISS manager Don McGhee. When Sidoti took the stage on that Tuesday night and played some Van Halen songs, Langston called Sexson.

"Richie, get down here," Langston said. "You have to hear this guy on guitar."

Sexson had already driven home after the game. It was late. He politely declined. So Langston invited Sidoti to the ballpark the following afternoon for a tour and to meet the team. Charles Nagy, Sandy Alomar Jr., and Manny Ramirez greeted Sidoti upon his arrival. Sidoti wore a Vizquel No. 13 jersey with a 1995 World Series patch. Langston led him to the dugout, where Vizquel was sitting on the bench.

"Hey," Langston said to his rock 'n' roll–loving teammate, "this is my friend, Paul. He's a guitar player."

Vizquel briefly acknowledged them before he scampered up the dugout steps to take infield practice. When he returned, he showed

Sidoti around the home clubhouse and the batting cages. They retreated to Vizquel's locker and Sidoti sat in the All-Star's chair.

"Where'd you get my jersey?" Vizquel asked him.

"I ordered it from the team shop when you guys were in the World Series," Sidoti replied.

"Man, that's really cool," Vizquel said. "I didn't even get to keep mine. They gave it to charity or something."

When Vizquel wasn't looking, Sidoti removed his jersey and stuffed it in the shortstop's locker. Langston directed them to a dressing room for clubhouse management staff, where a group of players had set up an area with a guitar and an amp for Sidoti to entertain. The players requested Eddie Van Halen's "Eruption," a demanding, 102-second masterpiece.

"I'm like, 'Oh, great,'" Sidoti said. "Right out of the gate, they want me to do something like that, without even warming up."

"You could bark out any song," Langston said. "He could play anything."

As Sidoti strummed the guitar, Vizquel sat beside him, grinning and motioning with his fingers on his own imaginary instrument.

"He gets up on the bench," Sidoti said, "and he does these David Lee Roth splits off the bench."

Then Vizquel shouted, "Tell Grover I'm not playing tonight! I'm going home to get my drums!"

Vizquel vanished for a minute, and Sidoti kept playing. Eventually, the shortstop returned, holding the jersey he discovered in his locker.

"I really appreciate you wanting to give me my jersey back," he told Sidoti. "I don't need it."

He handed it to Sidoti. Vizquel had scribbled a message on the front of the uniform.

To my amigo, Paul: Let's jam.—Omar Vizquel

"From that point on," Sidoti said, "we just had a real kinship."

One day, Sidoti called his dad to provide a warning.

"Hey dad, I have Omar Vizquel and a couple of the other guys on the Indians coming over to jam tonight after the game."

"No way."

"I'm serious. We're coming over."

Sidoti stored a drum kit in his parents' basement. That night, he hopped in Vizquel's famed Porsche, parted the sea of fans camping outside the players' parking lot—"They screamed like they were the Beatles," Sidoti said—and sped toward his parents' house in Strongsville. Sidoti opened the front door and his dad was standing there, in awe. The next time Sidoti hosted a player-driven jam session, his dad ordered deli trays and assembled an impressive beer stash. His mom cooked everyone pasta from time to time.

When Vizquel injured his knee in 2003, he and Sidoti played music all summer. Sidoti helped Vizquel box up autographed bats for season-ticket holders. Vizquel watched Sidoti's KISS tribute band perform in Akron. When Sidoti worked for KISS, their tour opened at Dodger Stadium on Halloween night. Sidoti gifted Vizquel a T-shirt featuring the four original band members donning Dodgers jerseys. When Vizquel attended Sidoti's tribute band performance, he sported that T-shirt and snapped photos of the band as the members applied the patented black and white face paint.

"I collect a lot of KISS stuff," Vizquel said. "I love KISS. I used to have my bedroom full of KISS stuff all over the place."

Sidoti has vivid memories of Vizquel donning his Ace Frehley wig while playing the drums. Vizquel still possesses a small camcorder with old videos of the two of them jamming together in that basement. Sidoti would strike the first few notes on his guitar, and Vizquel would follow on the drums. After a few minutes, they would be off the rails on a crazy train.

Sidoti eventually joined Taylor Swift's band, and when the musician and baseball player happened to cross paths in a particular city, they would link up. Sidoti would visit batting practice. Vizquel would attend a concert. During a trip to Minneapolis in 2011, when Vizquel played for the Chicago White Sox at the tail end of his career, Swift was performing in St. Paul. Sidoti had not checked the baseball schedule, but following an afternoon sound check, he noticed a voicemail alert on his phone.

"Hey, Paul, this is Omar. I'm looking out my hotel and I see all these girls dressed like Taylor Swift. You're in town, man! Give me a call!"

They spent the next afternoon catching up at Target Field. Vizquel described it as "a perfect friendship," originating from their love of baseball and music, from their endless supply of energy and from the parallels between two jobs that require them to be on the road quite frequently and to perform before tens of thousands of passionate fans.

"I always feel like I'm a 15-year-old kid when I'm around him," Sidoti said, "and I'm sure he feels that way, too.

"He's the life of the party."

That's how it was in 1995, too. Vizquel would leave the ballpark and trek to a local dive to nod along to some live music. Occasionally, he would hop up on stage and grab a microphone.

Really, nothing has changed in that regard. Vizquel still locates local hangouts and art galleries and concert venues. He frequented local art districts and wineries when he managed the White Sox A-ball affiliate in Winston-Salem in 2018. He is always buzzing around town in search of some activity to captivate his mind. He gets restless if he remains in his home, unless he is painting.

"Omar was a fun guy," Baerga said. "Omar was smiling all the time. If he went 0-for-10, 0-for-15, 0-for-20, he was the same person. That's something that I respect about him. Not too many people take it that way. A lot of people become crazy and put it in their mind and bring it to the infield."

Said Vizquel, "I always had that kind of personality. You can tell that I was enjoying what I was doing out there on the field. It didn't take long for people to realize, 'Hey, this guy is really enjoying his job.' That's just the way it is. Everybody was kind of intimidated or something. I didn't even speak English, but I was the one screaming and whistling and getting everybody going, 'Come on! Hey, let's go! Ahhh!' And being loud. When you show that to everybody, I think there's a pretty good chance people are going to notice you."

* * *

The Indians had a locker room full of colorful personalities in 1995. Vizquel was not the only one with musical interests. There was always a tune blaring throughout the clubhouse in the afternoon (and, of course, after wins).

"Oh, it was fun," Baerga said. "The music, the way we prepared ourselves, the way we stepped onto the field, the way we stretched and hit, it was different, very different. It was special."

Lofton said he sometimes felt sorry for manager Mike Hargrove, for having to deal with "Albert Belle's attitude," "my wildness all over the place," and the other cast of characters who kept the room lively. Lofton described it as a "wild frat house," which Hargrove would occasionally enter, shake his head, and walk right back out.

"The thing about the personalities was that you had a manager who allowed the guys to be themselves," Lofton said. "He would walk in the clubhouse and he would see the craziness and he would just walk out, because he knew that's who we were. We were something else. But when we got on the field, he knew the direction we were going to go to do our job. So he didn't make a big deal about the clubhouse being quieter. What for? He felt like, 'This is your second home away from home.' Why destroy that? Sometimes you would come in here and be like, 'Oh, God.' He would walk in and turn right back around. What are you going to do? Are you going to stop people from enjoying themselves? If we didn't perform on the field, then he probably would have something to say. But if you put up numbers on the field like we did—[he would] come into the clubhouse and say, 'Okay, you're not doing crazy stuff on the field. This is your guys' clubhouse. This is not someone else's clubhouse.' So we all respected that he just let us be."

And that is the key—work came first. Belle, Thome, and Ramirez spent hours in the batting cages with hitting coach Charlie Manuel. The pitchers spent plenty of time together dissecting scouting reports.

"Everybody was chilled out," Sandy Alomar Jr. said. "They said we were a crazy bunch, but everybody was prepared and knew what they were going to do and had a plan. It wasn't, like, out of control. It was just, yeah, we are normal people, normal young guys, injected with a few other veteran guys, and we do what kids do. We have fun, listen to music, and when we go out there between the lines, we kick butt. That's the bottom line. At times, it rubbed other teams the wrong way, because there was a lot of flair and dramatic stuff that we were doing and I don't think they liked it. But that's the confidence we had in ourselves."

Hargrove maintained a rule: once the clock struck 6:00 PM, the players were on "Grover's time."

"Essentially saying, 'We knew how much time we had before it was time to work.' They did a good job keeping it to that," Hargrove said.

Hargrove relied on Murray, Alomar, and Charles Nagy to keep peace in the clubhouse. Baerga mentioned Espinoza and Kirby as two key ingredients, two bench players who kept everyone in line. Of course, Espinoza was also known to plant giant, pink, bubble-gum balloons atop his teammates' caps.

"They let you know if you were trying to be, like, suave," Baerga said. "'No, no, no, no, no. Let's go! We have to play! We have to beat these guys!' They always kept you in line. You need leaders like that on a team."

Hargrove, though, was the one ultimately pulling the levers behind the scenes. The talent on the roster could translate to victories, sure, but Hargrove had to ensure that a clubhouse oozing with ego did not collapse.

"Every day you come to the ballpark, there are going to be fires to put out," Hargrove said. "As long as I stayed ahead of those fires— they did a great job. Obviously, you looked ahead to make sure things are going to go smoothly. But the longer they go smooth, the less you look for trouble. Usually if you look for trouble, you'll find it. It's easy enough; trouble will find you."

Alomar recalled, "[Hargrove] was awesome. He did a great job allocating responsibility to each guy. He let the guys play, pretty much, and let the players police themselves. If something got out of hand, he handled it. But he pretty much let the players police themselves. We had a good enough group that we could do that."

"These guys had a unique ability to be bouncing off the walls and come 7 o'clock, they left that behind and played the game," Hargrove said. "They played the game the way it was supposed to be played. It was interesting at times, but they all did a good job. I think they really enjoyed playing with each other."

"This Was About More Than Baseball. This Was About Life."

Mike Hargrove took over at the helm of the Indians for John McNamara in 1991 and faced the most challenging task of his career two years later.

There was no social media in 1993. Players' thumbs were not attached to cell phones. Sandy Alomar Jr. and Jim Thome were in their spring training apartment when Kenny Lofton sprinted to their door and started banging. Lofton rambled on and on, his words escaping his mouth at the speed with which he swiped a base, about Steve Olin and Tim Crews and a boating accident and how they were killed and—

Alomar finally interjected.

"I'm like, 'Dude slow down,'" Alomar said. "'What's going on?'"

Lofton explained what he knew. Olin and Crews, a couple of Indians relievers, had been killed in a boating accident on Little Lake Nellie, less than an hour north of Winter Haven, Florida.

"Tim Crews was a new teammate at that time. We didn't know him very well," Alomar said. "Bobby Ojeda was on the boat and he was alive. Fernando Montes, I was very close to Fernando, because he really helped me in my career with rehab and stuff like that. We became good friends. He had lost a draw to take the boat for a spin, so he was alive. But he was traumatized. One of the guys who was very close to me got away from that. It was just weird to see my teammates go. It was hard to get over that hump, too, in '93, especially when we were still rebuilding. But this was about more than baseball. This was about life. It was hard for us to see guys who had such a bright future in our organization go all of a sudden."

The tragedy took place on the only off day on the Indians' spring schedule. The Dodgers had offered to make up a rained-out affair that day, but Hargrove declined, knowing his players would prefer the time away from the facility. Crews, the new guy on the team, hosted some others, including the Olins, at his ranch.

Upon hearing the news, Nagy dashed to the Olins' apartment. Eventually, eight or nine people sat there, tears streaming down every face. The Indians' brass met at the office at 4:30 AM to sketch out a timeline. They held a morning press conference and planned to hold another one every few hours to keep the public informed and to prevent reporters from scavenging for information. Hargrove and general manager John Hart addressed the media first. Then Hargrove met with the team as players filed in for what would have been a regular game day. Some had no idea what had happened. They noticed the TV trucks and thought the Indians had pulled off a blockbuster trade. Then they saw the tears. In all, the Indians held four press conferences. Baerga represented the position players at one, and the entire bullpen sat together for another.

The Dodgers joined the Indians for a memorial service in a small auditorium in Winter Haven. The front office debated how soon the team should return to the field. The regular season was less than two weeks away. Team president Hank Peters suggested the club return to action swiftly rather than sit around and sulk. Hargrove countered that the players needed time to grieve. They returned to the field a couple of days after the tragedy, and on Opening Day—the last one at Municipal Stadium—the team sported a jersey patch to commemorate their late teammates. They also presented neatly folded jerseys to the two widows during a pregame ceremony.

The Indians started the '93 season with 15 losses in their first 22 games en route to a 76–86 finish in the final season at their old venue.

"We were digging out of a dark cloud for the whole first half of the season," said Dan O'Dowd.

When the Indians clinched the division in 1995, per Hargrove's request, the team honored Olin and Crews and, as they raised the American League Central banner in center field, the ballpark speakers blared "The Dance," the Garth Brooks song that Olin loved. Minutes after securing a long-awaited accomplishment, Indians players were bawling. It was the most difficult task of Hargrove's career, navigating a young team through an unthinkable tragedy.

8

"Pure Force and Power"

HANK PETERS SUMMONED DAN O'DOWD to his office one day. Peters, the team president, supplied O'Dowd, the director of player development, with a simple directive.

Dan, I think it's time we cut ties with Albert.

This was not so much a friendly suggestion as it was an ironclad order. Peters was not planning on engaging in a thoughtful debate about the issue. Albert Belle had whipped a baseball at a bothersome fan who had teased the left fielder about attending his keg party. Belle had spent two months the previous summer in an alcohol rehabilitation program at the Cleveland Clinic. His throw left a welt on the man's chest, earned him a suspension and a fine, and earned the Indians another headache.

The 1991 season was Belle's first full year in the majors, and another chapter in a *War and Peace*–length novel full of his Cleveland triumphs and troubles. As he aged, his anger-fueled antics did not subside. There was the infamous corked bat incident, the berating of reporters—including a verbal outburst toward NBC's Hannah Storm before Game 3 of the '95 World Series, an incident that resulted in a $50,000 fine—and his Halloween night chase-down of some egg-heaving trick-or-treaters. In the earlier stages of Belle's career, O'Dowd, the overseer of the Indians' farm system, often had to play mediator/babysitter. He shook his head when Belle destroyed a club-house sink while playing at Triple-A Colorado Springs. O'Dowd cooked up suspensions. He took phone calls from Belle's mother.

O'Dowd could rattle off the name of every promising prospect in the organization…and it would not take him very long. Only a few seconds, in fact, since the list was about 11 letters long.

A-L-B-E-R-T B-E-L-L-E.

The Indians employed some relatively intriguing young players but no one who came remotely close to possessing Belle's potential.

"In '89, '90, we did not have much talent at all," O'Dowd said. "We started to get talent as we got into '92, '93. Our drafts started to get a lot better and we started to accumulate talent."

The plan was to construct a winner that could emerge as a contender in conjunction with the opening of Jacobs Field in 1994. Kicking Belle to the curb certainly would not aid that cause. So O'Dowd challenged Peters.

"Hank, we can't cut ties with Albert," O'Dowd fired back.

That did not go over too well.

"I'm not asking you," Peters said. "I'm telling you. It's time to cut ties with Albert."

The Indians selected Belle in the second round of the 1987 amateur draft out of LSU. He did nothing but crush minor-league pitching, and he received his first promotion to the big leagues in 1989, when he spent the second half of the season with the Indians. In '91, Belle batted .282 with 28 home runs, 95 RBIs, 31 doubles, and an .863 OPS in 123 games with Cleveland. At that point, the Indians hadn't yet traded for Kenny Lofton. They didn't have Omar Vizquel or Eddie Murray. Jim Thome was a well-regarded infield prospect, but he didn't even reach the legal drinking age until late that summer, and he was as thin as a twig. The Indians drafted Manny Ramirez in the first round that June, but he was a few years away from joining Mike Hargrove's lineup on a regular basis.

Belle seemed like the surest thing, the possible batting order centerpiece, if he could stay on the field and stay out of the headlines.

So O'Dowd stuck to his guns.

"Hank, we're not cutting ties with Albert," he said. "He's the only prospect we have."

Peters looked O'Dowd in the eye.

"Okay," Peters said, "well, the next time I tell you to cut ties with Albert, I'm cutting ties with you, too."

Gulp.

O'Dowd walked out of his boss' office with a sinking feeling in his stomach. His fate was now tied to that of a completely unpredictable man. O'Dowd won the battle, but his prospects of winning the war did not seem promising. Neither were the prospects in the Indians system, though, so O'Dowd kept telling himself he took the proper stance.

Paul Shuey made his major league debut in Baltimore on May 8, 1994, a breezy Sunday afternoon at Camden Yards. Shuey entered in the eighth inning, the Indians trailing by an 8–6 margin. His first adversary, Mark McLemore, worked the count full before sending a broken-bat liner to left field. Shuey was expecting the baseball to plunge to the outfield grass for a bloop single, but Belle dashed in and made a sliding catch.

"Somebody came up to me," Shuey said, "and was like, 'I've never seen him slide to make a catch. That was big.' So it was one of those things where I had the utmost respect for the man. I liked the way he went about his business. I know if I was a media guy, it would not have been fun. But I wasn't. I was a teammate and he was a fantastic teammate. He had his routine. He was structured. He knew exactly what he was looking for. He was a very, very smart man, a very, very smart baseball man. He was very prepared. And I learned a lot: 'This is what you need to do. You need to have a routine where you go out and perform day in and day out.'"

Every season, Belle's numbers improved.

1992: Belle played his first complete season in the majors, appearing in 153 games, belting 34 home runs and tallying 112 RBIs. He finished 23rd in the voting for American League Most Valuable Player.

1993: Belle earned his first All-Star Game trip and Silver Slugger Award. He clubbed 38 home runs, led the league with 129 RBIs, stole a career-best 23 bases, greatly reduced his strikeout rate, and posted a .290/.370/.552 slash line. He totaled 77 extra-base hits and finished seventh in the AL MVP balloting.

1994: Perhaps Belle's most prolific season, but it tends to get lost in the shuffle because of the players' strike. Belle recorded a jarring .357/.438/.714 slash line, with 36 home runs and 35 doubles in only 106 games. He led the league with 294 total bases, collected another All-Star Game nod and Silver Slugger Award, and finished third in the AL MVP voting.

1995: This was Belle's coronation as the most fearsome hitter in baseball. Or, at least, the AL MVP Award should have symbolized as much. Instead, he finished second to Mo Vaughn, whose respectable numbers paled in comparison. Many point to Belle's contentious relationship with the media as the reason for his unjustified silver medal. Belle became the only player in big-league history to rack up 50 doubles and 50 home runs in a single season. He totaled 103 extra-base hits, 121 runs, 126 RBIs, and nearly as many walks (73) as strikeouts (80), to go along with a .317/.401/.690 slash line. All of that in only 143 games, too. His 377 total bases led the league, and his production merited him a third consecutive All-Star Game appearance and Silver Slugger Award.

"He was a gamer," Sandy Alomar Jr. said. "He would come in and nobody could outwork Albert with hitting. He was prepared. He would log every pitch he saw from every pitcher. He would study those logs, how guys pitch to him, and next time he would face them, he would set the guy up. So he was as prepared as anybody I have ever seen when it comes to hitting. The guy did well because the guy prepared and worked hard. All of his preparation and initiative to get ready for the game was a little different than everybody else, a little intense at times, but he never disrespected his teammates or anything like that.

"He just went about his business and you have to respect a guy who goes about his business by doing the best he can so we could win. I have nothing but respect for his work ethic and for going out there and playing the game the right way."

Belle still keeps note cards in his garage that detail his battles with various pitchers. He treated each at-bat as a winner-take-all match, and he developed an intricate routine—hours in the batting cages, hours studying those notes—that helped him prepare for each game.

"For the most part, he was a good teammate," Hargrove said. "He really was. He was the ultimate competitor. He wanted to win. He wanted to be the best that night, the next night, the night after that. At season's end, he wanted to be the best."

By 1995, he was. He batted fourth in Hargrove's Lineup of Terror, but he was the one guy no pitcher wanted to face in any sort of high-leverage situation. He stepped into the batter's box with a menacing glare and gripped the bat in a daunting way, hunched over, the lumber hovering over the plate until he was ready to pounce. He wanted to punish every pitch. There were no bloops or soft tappers when he uncorked a mighty swing.

"Albert was just pure force and power," O'Dowd said.

The surly, oft-scowling slugger earned the nickname Mr. Freeze after he grumbled about the temperature in the clubhouse. Belle would say that Lofton was notoriously cold at all times. Lofton would counter that he thought Belle had menopause, because Belle was always uncomfortably hot. As Lofton tells the story, Belle one day turned on the air conditioning in the clubhouse and set it to 40 degrees. That made Lofton frigid and frustrated, so the center fielder changed the temperature to somewhere in the 75- to 80-degree range. That irked Belle, who turned it back down to 40. After three or four games of cat and mouse, Belle, bat in hand, lowered the temperature to 35 degrees. And then he smashed the device. For two days, Lofton said, players walked around the clubhouse while sporting the oversized, puffy jackets typically only seen on idle pitchers in April or October.

As Omar Vizquel started his managerial career in the Chicago White Sox minor-league system, his players would ask him about memorable teammates from his playing days. Vizquel would mention the fierce competitors "with the strongest personalities, the guys who were dictating the pace in those days." And that was Belle.

"[Albert] would wrinkle his nose up like freakin' Mike Tyson, like, on every pitch," said pitching coach Mark Wiley. "I've never seen a guy that intense. He didn't give at-bats away. He was a beast that didn't give at-bats away. Think about that: Manny [Ramirez] used to sit on pitches and he would take three strikes in a row because the guy never threw the pitch that he wanted, and he would just walk back to the dugout. It didn't matter if it was bases loaded or whatever it was.

He would walk back to the dugout. Other guys would get anxious and over-swing early with runners in scoring position.

"Albert was a beast. He was on the attack all the time, and he never let up. And he played every inning, all the time. He had some quirks—big-time quirks and some weird stuff and some temper tantrums. But I always used to tell guys [that] the thing about Albert is that our guys grew up with him. They grew up with him in the minor leagues and played with him in the big leagues. They knew Albert and they knew what his quirks were.

"I'll never forget it. I still laugh. We had a new guy on the team and Albert made an out. He came down and goes down the tunnel and you hear an unbelievable explosion. He threw a bat through a wall or something. This new guy goes, 'What the hell was that?' And I remember Sandy said, 'Ah, it's just Albert. Don't worry about him.' It never took the focus away from our team, anything that Albert did, because they knew him and they just said, 'Oh, that's Albert. Who cares? He's an idiot. Who cares?' They would make comments like that, but they didn't let it bother them or lose their focus. And I think that had a lot to do with them growing up with him. We used to laugh—'I wonder how it's going to be with Frank Thomas when he goes over to the White Sox? I wonder, when he's throwing bats into walls and stuff, if it's going to take the focus away from their guys.'"

The Home Run Derby

Belle was the heartbeat of the Indians' lineup in 1995. He entered the midseason break with a .312 average and a .969 OPS, which warranted him the start in left field for the AL in the 66th All-Star Game. Belle batted fifth, with teammates Lofton and Carlos Baerga occupying the top two spots in Buck Showalter's lineup in Arlington,

Texas. Dennis Martínez and Jose Mesa both pitched in the game and Ramirez walked twice, giving the Indians six All-Star representatives, their most since 1955, when there were eight American League teams.

Belle and Lofton each went hitless in three at-bats in the annual exhibition. Baerga notched a double and a pair of singles—as many hits as the National League totaled as a team—in his three trips to the plate. He could have been in line to claim the game's MVP honors if not for Jeff Conine's go-ahead home run in the eighth inning, which vaulted the NL to victory.

Belle and Ramirez both participated in the Home Run Derby the afternoon before the Midsummer Classic. On the ESPN broadcast, Chris Berman joked that the entire Indians lineup could have partaken in the festivities, given the club's offensive proficiency. Pundits were bullish that a right-handed hitter would have to win the contest, given the ballpark's dimensions, the daunting left-field wall, and the way the ball often failed to carry to that side of the stadium. Mo Vaughn was the only left-handed hitter among the eight competitors, with Frank Thomas, Ron Gant, Raul Mondesi, Sammy Sosa, and Reggie Sanders rounding out the field.

Belle participated in the competition the previous two years but totaled only five home runs. He only joined the fray in '95 because Mark McGwire had to withdraw after being struck on the helmet by a pitch two days earlier. Belle didn't even know he would be among the contestants until he arrived in Arlington the night before. The temperature on the field soared north of 120 degrees on the sunny, summer afternoon. Thomas joked after the second round that he was out of gas but would feel fine once he ate a Snickers bar.

Players received 10 outs in the first two rounds, an out representing any swing that did not produce a home run. Belle recorded three outs to start his opening round… and then he started to pepper the second deck in left field. He totaled seven home runs in his first session. Ramirez hit three, the final one barely sneaking over the fence in right center field. He had started to walk away from the batter's box, thinking he had logged his last out, until the baseball disappeared. Still, he finished tied for fourth after the first round and lost the tie-breaker to Gant. With one out remaining, Thomas belted two home runs to surpass Belle's leading total.

Belle needed three home runs in the second round to advance to the finals, but he only had one home run with one out remaining. So he launched a baseball beyond the "I Can't Believe It's Yogurt" advertisement in left field. Then he launched one off the left field foul pole. He launched one to the second deck in left. Then he launched one into the bullpen. He launched one that caromed off of the facing of the second deck. Then he launched one to the second deck just inside the foul pole. On the broadcast, Joe Morgan quipped, "You know what? He better save some of those." He was right. Lofton brought Belle a cup of water and a towel.

"When Albert gets loose," Lofton told Buck Martinez on the broadcast, "he starts to turn it on, and that's what he did. Once he got loose, it was over." Martinez asked if Belle could "go all the way." "Yeah," Lofton said. "It's over. Frank has no chance now."

Belle looked at Lofton and joked, "I think I stiffened up too much in the AC down in the locker room. I have to stay out here and stay warm."

Belle and Thomas squared off in the finals, with each player receiving only five outs. Belle's first home run ricocheted off the left field foul pole, prompting Thomas to say, "He's got that pole down." Belle only managed two home runs, and Thomas quickly tied him and then squeaked a liner over the wall in center. "I didn't think that last one was going to get out," he said, "but that's cool. I'll take it." Belle out-homered Thomas 16–15, but the White Sox slugger emerged victorious.

Though his numbers indicated otherwise, Belle said that he felt uncomfortable at the plate in the first half of the 1995 season, that he was missing on certain pitches he should have squared up. The Home Run Derby helped to get him in a better rhythm. After the All-Star break, Belle posted a 1.202 OPS, with 36 home runs, nearly one every other game. He walked more than he struck out, and he totaled 75 RBIs in 76 contests.

"Albert was kind of the guy we fed off of," Thome said. "When he was hitting, boy it was so much fun. He set the bar as a teammate so high. I think we carried that. We wanted to be as good of a player as he was."

The MVP Vote

Belle figured his numbers, no matter how gaudy, would probably not propel him to the AL MVP award in 1995. He even told *USA Today*, "It's going to be tough. I'm not really considered a media darling."

"He expected to get the big hit every single time," Paul Shuey said. "And he had 50 homers and 50 doubles. I mean, come on."

The tale of the tape favored Belle in just about every way imaginable, but the voting veered the other direction. Mo Vaughn received 12 first-place votes to Belle's 11. Overall, Vaughn tallied 308 points. Belle finished second, with 300. Seattle slugger Edgar Martínez finished third with 244 points, including four first-place nods. Jose Mesa garnered the final first-place vote. The Tribe closer finished fourth overall, with 130 points.

Belle trumped Vaughn in batting average (.317 to .300), on-base percentage (.401 to .388), slugging percentage (.690 to .575), runs scored (121 to 98), hits (173 to 165), home runs (50 to 49), and WAR (7.2 to 5.1). Each player racked up 126 RBIs.

"I saw so many home runs that year," Sandy Alomar Jr. said. "Fifty homers and 52 doubles. Every time he hit the ball, it seemed like he hit the ball right on the nose. There was a lot of noise from his bat. He was exciting to watch and to do what he did, 50 doubles and 50 homers, it's just unheard of."

Belle's march to 50 home runs was incredible in itself, considering he entered the month of August with only 19. In 58 games from August 1 to October 1, he batted .350 with an .885 slugging percentage, 31 home runs, 62 RBIs, 23 doubles, and 60 runs scored. He slugged a cool .929 over the final month, and he belted his 50th blast on the penultimate day of the regular season.

With Saturday afternoon shadows beginning to bear down on Jacobs Field, Belle deposited a fastball from Kansas City hurler Melvin Bunch onto the plaza in left field. The solo shot tied the game at 2–2, paving the way for the Indians' 10-inning victory. Belle dropped his bat and watched the baseball sail over the fence as he commenced his home run trot with his typical, stoic gaze. His teammates stood and clapped in the dugout. After he retreated to the bench, Belle stepped back out and acknowledged the fans with a curtain call, raising his right arm and pumping his fist. Slider, the team's furry, pink mascot, bowed down to Belle while standing atop the dugout. The fans refused to cease in their appreciation of Belle's feat, so the slugger stepped out of the dugout a second time, raised both of his arms above his head and pumped his fists.

"Every time he stepped to the plate," Charles Nagy said, "magic was going to happen."

9

Boston, Bulging Biceps, and a Late-Night Blast to the Bleachers

WHAT STANDS OUT MOST to Mike Hargrove a quarter-century later is how long the game lasted, deep into the night, hours past any early bird's bedtime and far beyond the expectations of anyone who spent the night (and, technically, morning) at the ballpark on a Tuesday. That Wednesday morning alarm would be a most unwelcome irritant.

"It was a long, cold, wet game," Hargrove said.

Five hours and one minute, to be precise, with the second hand's extra trip around the clock providing the most critical and, perhaps, the most unanticipated moment. The Indians' first postseason tilt in 41 years—the franchise's farewell to playing the role of league punching bag—featured everything: a couple of rain delays, a handful of dramatic home runs, extra innings. All of the customary elements of a memorable affair. Oh, and the opposing manager hollering at the umpires to check the bat of the slugger who had just launched a game-tying blast in the 11th. And, of course, the most memorable pose featuring the most renowned muscle in team history.

It all ended long after many had retired for the night, only a few hours before many rose for work. But why don't we back up for a minute.

The Indians piled up a major league–high 100 wins. They toppled the runners-up in the American League Central, the Kansas City Royals, by 30 games. No other AL squad finished within 14 games of the Indians. And yet, in their first playoff series since 1954, they did not benefit from home-field advantage. That privilege went to the Red Sox, Cleveland's opponent, who finished with the second-best record.

At the time, home-field advantage rotated each year so teams that shared their stadiums with their football counterparts could schedule games ahead of time. In 1995, the AL Central was the redheaded step-child. So the Red Sox and the AL West champion Mariners earned the extra home game in each playoff round. Another rule mandated that teams could not square off against a division foe in the opening round of the postseason. So the Wild Card–winning Yankees could not battle the Red Sox in the ALDS. That left the Indians to play the Red Sox and the Mariners to play the Yankees.

The Indians' reward for blitzing through their competition for five months at a historic pace? A date with the second-best team in their league. The 2–2–1 format had not been instituted yet. Instead, the Indians hosted the first two games. The final three contests would take place at Fenway Park, if necessary.

The Indians had no way of winning the series at Jacobs Field. And in Game 1, they had to face Roger Clemens, who was smack dab in the center of a career that included 11 All-Star Game nods and seven Cy Young Awards. Good luck.

The Indians countered with 41-year-old Dennis Martínez. Hargrove felt confident that Martínez, a master of pinpoint command, could limit Boston's lineup, which produced the second-best marks in the AL in batting average, on-base percentage, and slugging percentage—all behind the Indians, of course. He also was certain the

Indians would, at the very least, make Clemens work. Clemens issued nearly four walks per nine innings during the regular season, and Jim Thome, Albert Belle, and Manny Ramirez all drew more than 70 free passes.

A 39-minute rain delay forced the first pitch to 8:44 PM, around the time Baerga started barking, "We're going to kill you!" at Clemens from the dugout. It was already shaping up to be a late night, but no one had any inkling of the sequence of events that would ultimately unfold. The Indians finally broke through against Clemens in the sixth, as Belle delivered a two-out, two-run double and Eddie Murray followed with an RBI single. Luis Alicea socked a game-tying homer in the eighth off Julian Tavarez. Another rain shower paused the action for 23 minutes.

The teams proceeded into extra innings, tied at three. Tim Naehring gave the Red Sox a 4–3 edge with a solo shot off Jim Poole in the top of the 11th. Belle responded with one of his own to begin the bottom half of the inning. And then, the drama arrived.

Red Sox manager Kevin Kennedy requested that the umpires check Belle's bat for cork. Hart figured the Indians were in the Boston players' heads. The Red Sox thought the Indians were stealing signs. Major League Baseball officials had devoted their afternoon to inspecting Jacobs Field, searching for any illegal cameras or other forms of illicit baseball sorcery. Hart laughed off the accusations and referred to Murray and Carlos Baerga as wizards when it came to picking up signals. Charles Nagy thought Kennedy was attempting to throw Belle off his game.

There *was* precedent for such an allegation, even though the timing made the call to action a bit of an insulting stretch. Belle had previously corked his bats. It was not a secret in the Indians' clubhouse, and opponents had an inkling, too. On July 15, 1994, White

Sox skipper Gene Lamont received a tip about the matter before their game against Cleveland. The two teams had been jockeying back and forth atop the AL Central. Belle hit a home run the previous night and entered the Friday night meeting with an eye-opening .356/.443/.696 slash line. In the first inning, Lamont halted the action and approached umpire Dave Phillips to dispute the legality of Belle's lumber. Phillips confiscated the bat and stored it in his locker in the umpires' dressing room.

Jason Grimsley had the night off from pitching, so he concocted a master plan. He would embark on an adventure with one clear mission—retrieve Belle's bat and leave behind an impostor. After all, the Indians knew Belle's bat was not up to code, and they could not afford to lose their most imposing slugger for any period of time. Grimsley retreated to the clubhouse to survey the scene and solve what he termed a puzzle. The umpires' room was locked, so he needed a stealthy, unconventional route. He grabbed a flashlight and a bat belonging to Paul Sorrento. Why not simply replace one Belle bat with another Belle bat? Well, that is because all of his bats were corked, as Omar Vizquel would attest in his autobiography, published nearly nine years after the incident in Chicago (and two and a half years after Belle's final major league game).

Grimsley stepped up onto the desk in Hargrove's office, removed a ceiling tile, vaulted himself up into a narrow passageway and crawled toward what he thought was the umpires' room. At one point during his excursion, he lifted a ceiling panel and prepared to descend to the area beneath him. One problem—it was not the umpires' room. A groundskeeper sat on a couch below, so Grimsley returned the panel and continued along his route. He finally discovered the proper room, and he dropped to the refrigerator and then hopped to the floor. He had to move swiftly; if anyone caught him in the act—and, especially, in the locked room—he would be doomed. The bat was somewhat shielded in Phillips' locker, but Grimsley spotted it and switched in Sorrento's model, even though it displayed the first baseman's name. He certainly was not fooling anyone. Grimsley climbed back up into the ceiling, scurried to the Indians' clubhouse, and spread the word to his teammates in the dugout.

Mission accomplished. Well, sort of.

The Indians emerged victorious that night 3–2 against Chicago, but it did not take long for the umpires to notice the impropriety. Something about the name on the bat gave it away. Phillips was convinced someone had broken into the room. White Sox owner Jerry Reinsdorf dubbed the wrongdoing a "serious crime." The league immediately launched an investigation, and commissioner Bud Selig promised that they would "get to the bottom of this." Ultimately, the league struck an agreement with the Indians. The intruder could remain anonymous if the club delivered Belle's original bat to the American League office. The Indians complied and Belle received a 10-game suspension, which was trimmed to seven games after an appeal. Grimsley waited about five years before he detailed his escapades to the *New York Times*.

But back to that October night—well, technically, morning—15 months later. The umpires seized the bat and sawed it open after the game. No cork. That did not surprise anyone in Cleveland's dugout. They knew Belle's bats, at that point, contained nothing illegal.

Belle was furious. Hargrove was shouting at Kennedy from the home dugout and he was so enraged that he said he and Kennedy went several years without speaking after that night. Belle wanted to send the message that his hours in the weight room were responsible for the baseball's flight plan, not some external aid, so as he stood in the home dugout and shot a menacing glare across the field, he squeezed his right fist, flexed his biceps, and pointed to the bulging muscle as his uniform sleeve hung on for dear life. As Belle shouted at Kennedy, veins protruded from his right forearm and his eyebrows curled. Surely, that visual snuck its way into the nightmares of some members of the Red Sox that winter.

Nearly two decades later, Indians vice president of public affairs Bob DiBiasio asked Belle to grant his approval on the team creating a bobblehead in his likeness. "It's about time!" Belle responded. Before DiBiasio could utter another word, Belle requested that the ceramic model pose in that flexing stance. The Indians obliged.

With the clock ticking past 2:00 AM on that soggy night, broad-casters Bob Costas and Bob Uecker, likely fueled by a few cups of coffee, had engaged in some off-topic storytelling. They were not the only ones in need of some caffeine. DiBiasio and team broadcaster Rick Manning were poking around the Indians' clubhouse, seeking some hot tea or Pepsi, anything they could find—save for coffee, which DiBiasio did not drink—that would offer a late-night energy boost. Their search was interrupted by a stampede of players who had shifted their on-field celebration to the home clubhouse.

Costas was taking light-hearted jabs at Uecker's unheralded playing career as Red Sox reliever Zane Smith misfired with his first three offerings to 38-year-old Tony Peña. Typically, Peña served as Martínez's personal catcher, but Hargrove elected to start Sandy Alomar Jr. in Game 1, since Alomar was the more capable offen-sive contributor and Clemens could make life difficult on any lineup. Alomar was lifted for a pinch-runner in the 10th inning, so Peña entered the game in the 11th.

Hargrove usually granted his hitters permission to swing away on a 3–0 count, unless a particular situation dictated that it might be advantageous to challenge the pitcher to find the strike zone. Hitting coach Charlie Manuel could stomach a hitter swinging at a 3–0 pitch, but he maintained certain guidelines.

"Don't be God damn hitting it the other way, shaving it into the dugout on the other side of the field," Manuel said. "We've earned the right to swing the bat when it's 3–0."

Hargrove joked that Peña was even slower than the manager was, and that it might require two doubles to score him from first if he walked. So there was incentive to allow the catcher to take a hack, even with the hitter's count. But when asked after the game if he gave Peña a green light or a red light, Hargrove quipped that it "was more amber than anything else."

Peña said third-base coach Jeff Newman delivered a take sign, but Peña had a hunch that he should swing and that Smith might just try to get over a strike to battle back in the at-bat. Uecker was mid-sentence when Costas cut him off and shrieked, "Oh man! Oh man! Tony Peña! On 3-and-0! Sends everybody home!" Costas and Uecker never finished their late-night tale.

Peña immediately flipped his bat away, toward the Indians' dugout. The baseball settled in the first row of the bleachers, perched above the 19-foot-high wall in left field. A group of fans clad in orange ponchos chased after the ball as Peña raised both arms in the air and circled the bases. He slapped hands with Baerga and then entered a mosh pit at home plate.

"That was a key game for us to believe that, 'Hey, we can go through Boston, no problem,'" Alomar said.

Tom Hamilton shouted on the radio broadcast, "Tenth time this year they've ended a game here with a home run, and probably the last person in the park you would think would take a 3–0 pitch and get the green light!"

Peña was a five-time All-Star and a four-time Gold Glove Award winner, but by that juncture in his career, his primary tasks were to guide the pitchers through the game and to hold down the fort while Alomar worked his way back from knee surgery. Still, despite all he accomplished—he also appeared in a pair of World Series—Peña points to that home run as the highlight of his career.

It proved to be a critical victory for the Indians, given the series' scheduling quirks, and it made for a momentous way to secure their first playoff win in 47 years. The Indians rode that momentum to a three-game sweep. The teams returned to Jacobs Field the next night and played a tidy, two-hour, 33-minute game in which Orel Hershiser silenced Boston's bats for a 4–0 win. The teams combined for seven hits, the two most impactful being an Omar Vizquel two-run double in the fifth and a two-run home run by Murray in the eighth.

Before the Indians boarded the team bus to head to Fenway Park for Game 3, they completed one other task: they checked out of the team hotel. There was no doubt in their minds that they would be flying back to Cleveland at the end of the night, rather than returning to their high-rise for another crack at the continental breakfast the next morning.

Cleveland's hitters knocked around knuckleballer Tim Wakefield in Game 3, and Charles Nagy—a native of New England who grew up in Bridgeport, Connecticut, and attended the University of Connecticut—limited the Red Sox lineup to one run over seven innings. Paul Assenmacher pitched a scoreless ninth to seal the 8–2 triumph. Mo Vaughn, the league MVP, and Jose Canseco, his companion in the middle of Boston's order, combined to go hitless in 27 at-bats in the series. A matchup of the top two offenses in the league resulted in a power outage.

Red Sox during the regular season: .280 average, .812 OPS
Red Sox during the AL Division Series: .184 average, .535 OPS
Indians during the regular season: .291 average, .839 OPS
Indians during the AL Division Series: .219 average, .698 OPS

As Belle fittingly squeezed his glove to secure the final fly ball, Vizquel jumped into his arms. Their teammates and coaches spilled out of the dugout in a deliberate, tame manner, and the Indians celebrated their advancement to the AL Championship Series, one step from their first World Series appearance since 1954.

"It was really unbelievable," said pitching coach Mark Wiley recently. "I can only imagine what it was like when Boston won their first World Series after all those years. I think the people of Cleveland and all of baseball, they knew that we were one of the elite teams and the fact that we went all the way through and we were so good and we basically went wire to wire, there still was that relief when you finally close the door and you actually can move on to the playoffs and you've won something. And then, of course, when Tony won that first playoff game with the home run in extra innings against Boston, that went right along with what we had done all year. It was unbelievable. Everything seemed to come together."

Five Other Slightly Less Iconic Poses in Progressive Field Lore

Albert Belle's biceps flex stands out as perhaps the defining stance in team history, given its timing and its blend of braggadocio and intimidation. What other body parts received such a spotlight? (No, Grady Sizemore fans, we are not talking about those hidden behind a coffee mug.) Trevor Bauer's right pinkie, dripping blood like a leaky faucet during Game 3 of the 2016 ALCS, comes to mind. So, too, does Bob Feller's right arm, which was put on display from a young age, as Feller was plastered onto the cover of magazines and was asked to fire a baseball faster than a speeding motorcycle in an effort to showcase his talent.

Belle's pose, though—the anger and adrenaline coursing through his veins—is as iconic as it gets. Here are a handful of other memorable Indians poses since Belle's unforgettable flex.

Kenny's Catch
The pose: Kenny Lofton's back turned toward the field of play, his arm hanging over the green fence in center field, his right spike digging into the horizontal ledge halfway up the wall

The backstory: Sandy Alomar Jr. was warming up Eric Plunk in the bullpen when he "heard a boom." He peered up from his crouched stance and there was Lofton, his armpit resting atop the fence, the baseball resting in his glove. On August 4, 1996, the Indians led the Orioles 3–2 in the eighth inning at Jacobs Field. Paul Shuey served up a single to Rafael Palmeiro and struck out Bobby Bonilla. B.J. Surhoff tattooed a 3–0 fastball to center field and Lofton took off. Omar Vizquel, standing at shortstop, said he thought the ball would sail over the wall without issue.

"I dropped my head," Vizquel said, "and I said, 'Damn, man.'"

But Lofton was a former basketball player who starred at the University of Arizona. He won his fourth Gold Glove Award in 1996. He possessed plenty of athleticism, and he got a great jump when the ball connected with Surhoff's bat. He planted his foot on the padded ledge to prevent himself from sliding down the wall, and with his back turned toward the plate, he reached over the fence and hauled in the baseball. Years later, the Indians designed a bobblehead that depicted the catch.

Vizquel: "All of a sudden, I look and Kenny is coming out of nowhere. I'm like, 'Whoa. Oh, my God. I can't believe it.'"

Dennis Martínez: "I was in the dugout. I looked up and I go, 'Wow!' That was unbelievable."

Alomar: "I said, 'Holy shit! No way that just happened. That's impressive.'"

Jim Thome: "I was just in awe. I could not believe he made that catch.... It was one of the greatest catches I ever saw. Literally, I thought he was going to jump over the wall. The fact that he could even get there in time to do that was incredible."

Lofton: "I always ran hard and went after balls at the wall, because you never know. You can't catch it if you're not up there."

Keep Steady, Eddie

The pose: Eddie Taubensee's left hand holding Lofton's right knee and his right hand grasping Lofton's left leg, with the center fielder flung over his right shoulder

The backstory: Taubensee and Lofton were traded for each other in December 1991, but on August 5, 2001, Taubensee was waiting on deck as Jolbert Cabrera batted with Lofton on second and Omar Vizquel on first. The Indians had erased a 14–2 deficit with three runs in the seventh, four runs in the eighth, and five runs in the ninth, capped by Vizquel's two-out, bases-clearing triple down the right-field line. In the fifth inning, with the Indians trailing by 12 runs, hitting coach Charlie Manuel told Vizquel, "Get ready, because you're going to win this game." Vizquel replied by asking facetiously if he was going to hit a 10-run homer. It probably deserves to be mentioned that this all happened against the Seattle Mariners, who proceeded to tie a major league record with 116 wins that season.

"Boy, they probably would have loved to have that game," Taubensee said. "That would have put them over the top."

Mike Bacsik made his big-league debut that night in relief of Dave Burba, who surrendered seven runs over two innings. Bacsik allowed seven runs (six earned) but chewed up six innings to save Cleveland's bullpen. Bacsik had never met Jim Thome or Roberto Alomar or Travis Fryman, but he idolized each of them, and they all approached him to thank him for keeping the team in the game.

"I'm like, 'Man, I've never been congratulated for giving up seven runs in six innings,'" Bacsik said.

With the score tied at 14–14 in the 11th, Cabrera smacked a single to left, and Lofton scampered home with the winning run. After Lofton crossed the plate, Taubensee lifted him over his shoulder as their teammates darted toward the plate to celebrate. The Indians tied the major league record for largest comeback, a feat that had not been achieved in 75 years.

Taubensee: "I'm going home to help with the play at the plate, to tell him to get down, if needed. He got down and he jumped up, knowing that he scored and we won the game. It was just a natural reaction—I grabbed him and picked him up. He scored the winning run. I wanted to carry him around and celebrate."

Lofton: "I scored and the next thing you know, we're going crazy, like, 'This is going to be the comeback of the century.' It was pretty much that. Once I scored, I was like, 'Wow.'"

Vizquel: "I see the video once in a while and I can't believe that happened."

Taubensee: "It sends a lot of messages of perseverance, not quitting."

Thome: "It was surreal. It just proved that you never give up. There's never a time in the game where you should give up, and we proved it that night. If it's any learning lesson to a young kid, to a young team, it's, 'Hey, until that last out is made, you give it everything you've got.'"

Naquin's Rockin' Stance

The pose: Tyler Naquin standing tall above home plate, his right arm raised as he tilts backward and points his right index finger and pinkie toward the sky

The backstory: On August 13, 1916, Braggo Roth sunk the St. Louis Browns with a walk-off, inside-the-park home run at Dunn Field to vault the Indians to a 4–3 victory. Unfortunately, we could not unearth any photo evidence of the accomplishment to consider a snapshot of Roth's celebration for this list. But we did find *The Plain Dealer*'s description of the sequence of events:

He tensed every muscle and with his bat drawn back he swung with every ounce of his strength. Away sailed the ball. Center fielder [Armando] Marsans gave one look and then dashed for the score board. The Cuban is fleet of foot, but even his speed would not allow him to catch up with the ball, which traveled like a bullet and never stopped until it bounced against the score board. Roth was well past second when the Cuban picked it up. He never hesitated in rounding third and dashed home standing up as Marsans' throw to one of his mates who rushed into the field to ace as relay man went astray.

A veritable riot of enthusiasm ensued. Almost the entire tribe rushed to the plate to greet the great pinch hitter and slap him on the back as he rushed to the dugout. The joy of the Indians was but a sample of that displayed by the 18,000 rooters who were present. All they did was to cheer themselves hoarse, tear up their scorecards, toss their hats in the air and then go away forgetting wraps, canes, etc., in their excitement.

Nearly 100 years to the day of Roth's improbable accomplishment, Naquin duplicated the feat. He, too, tensed every muscle and, with his bat drawn back, swung with every ounce of his strength. Okay, there is probably a less antiquated way to recollect what happened on that Friday night in mid-August in 2016.

It started with José Ramírez, who tied the score at 2–2 with a solo home run to right field off Blue Jays closer Roberto Osuna in the ninth. Lonnie Chisenhall chased down teammate Chris Gimenez in the dugout and shouted, "He's prone!" Osuna entered the outing with a 1.84 ERA, but the Indians deemed him vulnerable.

Six weeks earlier, the Indians and Blue Jays needed 19 innings to settle a game in Toronto. The Indians emerged triumphant to secure their franchise-record (at the time) 14th consecutive win. But on this night, they did not want to advance to extra innings. They had played enough additional frames against Toronto.

Naquin finished third in the AL Rookie of the Year balloting in 2016. He had a knack for punishing breaking balls low in the zone. And Osuna threw him one. Naquin fouled it off. Assistant hitting coach Matt Quatraro was standing near the bat rack, hoping that Osuna would toss Naquin another one. He did.

What happened next? Let's allow former Tribe outfielder Rajai Davis to describe the sequence of events:

"When it goes up, it's like, 'It's a homer. For sure.' Then [right fielder Michael Saunders] goes back and it's like, 'Why is he setting up to catch the ball?' Then he's going to jump and catch it. 'Oh nooooo.' Then we see the ball come out. There's nobody there to back him up. 'Ohhhh. Yessss. Keep running. Keep running.' Then he gets to third. But the center fielder has the ball now. It's like,

'OK, he's out.' Then he slips. It's like, 'Wait a minute! You better send him! Keep going!' Everybody at that point that was on the field was sending him. We had to make sure he got down."

Naquin knew if the ball caromed far enough off the wall, he had a chance. And then center fielder B.J. Upton slipped while corralling the baseball. Naquin never hesitated, and he plunged, head-first, into home plate. A handful of teammates had rushed onto the field, thinking the ball would sail over the fence. They rushed back into the dugout, and then spilled back onto the field, guiding Naquin to the plate.

"We literally beat him there," Gimenez said. "That was the coolest part. I thought the umpire was going [to say something]."

Naquin bounced to his feet and struck the rock star pose, rocketing his right arm into the air before his teammates mauled him. Mike Napoli provided the most prolific pounding, sending Naquin's knees—and his face—to the dirt. Chisenhall carried a mostly empty tray of water cups to the pile while the rest of the players playfully pummeled the rookie.

"Just rockin' out," Naquin said. "That was a pretty cool moment, so I'm gonna get into it."

The next day, teammates tacked photoshopped pictures to the clubhouse bulletin board of Naquin racing Usain Bolt on the track and Michael Phelps in the pool.

"I watched [the replay] about 4 billion times," Gimenez said. "I didn't go to sleep until, like, 3:30 AM."

Rajai's Point to the Heavens

The pose: Rajai Davis' mouth wide open, his eyes wide, and his right arm and index finger raised in the air as he circles the bases

The backstory: How does a part-time outfielder leave a lasting impression upon an entire city after just one season with the franchise? How about a game-tying home run in Game 7 of the World Series, the sort of moment that still plops goosebumps onto any Indians fan's forearms when reviewing the video clip years after the fact.

Had the Indians emerged victorious in Game 7, had the champagne that had been wheeled into their clubhouse (before the brief rain delay that sapped them of their momentum) actually been sprayed throughout that plastic sheet-filled room, how would Davis be revered? Would his statue stand tall next to the depictions of Jim Thome and Bob Feller outside the center-field gates at Progressive Field? Francisco Lindor isn't so sure about that, but he guaranteed that Davis would be "eating for free for life in Cleveland."

Davis actually returned to the Indians' roster in 2018, but his tenure with the Tribe will forever be defined by the one swing, with his hands positioned several inches from the knob of the bat, against Aroldis Chapman on an unseasonably warm night in early November 2016. Lindor deemed it his "best experience in baseball," and that's coming from an energetic, young shortstop who reacts to a 6–3 putout like he just hopped off his favorite roller coaster at an amusement park.

Even though the Indians ultimately fell short against the Cubs, Davis' home run, which cleared the 19-foot-high left-field wall by only a few inches, remains one of the most unforgettable moments in team history. Chapman tossed him seven pitches in the at-bat, ranging from 98 mph to 101 mph. Davis fouled off four of the offerings until he yanked one thrown low and inside. Once the baseball disappeared—and it truly vanished; the Indians never got their hands on it to store in their archives—Davis raised his right arm and index finger as he rounded first base. He shouted, pounded his chest twice, and then returned his right arm to the air as he continued what was likely the quickest home run trot of his career.

"I'm glad I was a witness," Lindor said.

Davis said he has watched the replay enough times that he would be embarrassed to reveal the actual number.

"I'll definitely have a story to tell for the rest of my life, to my kids, to my family," he said.

Bruce's Torn Jersey

The pose: Jay Bruce, feet slightly off the ground, arms spread wide to absorb the oncoming tackles from Edwin Encarnacion, Francisco Lindor, and other teammates

The backstory: Somewhere in a dimly lit closet connected to a storage area in the bowels of Progressive Field rests a navy Indians uniform belonging to a player who spent a whopping two months with the team. The piping along the jersey's neckline is damaged, which is the primary reason the keepsake sits in that rarely visited room. On September 14, 2017, Jay Bruce's uniform survived a Gatorade downpour, splashes of water, and a baby powder shower.

"We were acting like kids," Josh Tomlin said. "You don't really know what you're doing in the moment. You just do it and you look back at it and say, 'Did I really do that? That was kind of weird.' But it's a lot of fun, too."

Bruce's uniform did *not* survive the smacking and tugging on the material, so it was never worn again. That is probably how it should have been, though. Bruce supplied a walk-off double that night to cap the Indians' 22–game winning streak, the modern-day major league record and the overall record, depending on how one views the 1916 New York Giants, who compiled a 26-game streak that included a tie.

By the end of the Indians' run, the media contingent covering the team on a daily basis had swelled. Players, coaches, front office members, and reporters received interview requests from national and international news outlets. Oddsmakers had vaulted the Indians to the top of the list of World Series favorites. The team shipped three items to the Baseball Hall of Fame: a baseball thrown by Corey Kluber during his complete-game shutout for win No. 20, Mike Clevinger's jersey worn in win No. 21, and second base from win No. 22. The team saved the last-out ball from wins 15 through 22, the lineup cards from wins 20 through 22, a Roberto Pérez bat and, of course, Bruce's uniform.

The win streak put the Indians in position to amass 100 wins in a season for the first time since 1995. And, really, the invincible stretch reminded many of the dominance that the 1995 team exhibited. During the streak, the Indians outscored the opposition by 105 runs. They posted a team ERA of 1.58. They also hit more home runs (41) than the opposition scored runs (37).

To push the streak to 22, Lindor delivered a game-tying RBI double off the left-field wall in the bottom of the ninth against the Royals. Bruce also delivered a walk-off double to right in the 10th.

"What we did was kind of crazy," said Indians reliever Dan Otero. "Three weeks without losing a freaking game. Looking back on it, it almost seems unattainable and history kind of proves that—it's never been done before. Maybe they'll make a movie out of us."

First baseman Eddie Murray joined the 3,000-hit club on June 30, 1995. Indians general manager John Hart and manager Mike Hargrove offered their congratulations.

The Indians had plenty of representation in the 1995 All-Star Game: second baseman Carlos Baerga (high-fiving fellow American League All-Star Frank Thomas of the White Sox), starters Albert Belle and Kenny Lofton, pitchers Denis Martinez and Jose Mesa, and reserve Manny Ramirez.

Pitcher Dennis Martinez was consistent and productive for the Indians in 1995, finishing in the league's top 10 in WAR (5th, 5.7), ERA (3rd), walks and hits per inning (3rd, 1.176), and home runs per nine innings (9th, 0.818).

The standout player of a standout 1995 season for the Indians was Albert Belle, who finished second in the AL MVP voting. Belle led the league in runs scored (121), runs batted in (126), doubles (52), home runs (50), total bases (377), and slugging percentage (.690).

Sandy Alomar Jr. didn't play his first game of the 1995 season until June 29...but the season he delivered for the team once he got going was worth the wait.

Mike Hargrove, in a shortened season, would lead the Indians to a 100–44 record in 1995.

The team celebrates (with mascot, Slider) after clinching the AL Central Division on September 8, 1995.

When Tony Peña hit the game-winning home run to defeat the Boston Red Sox 5–4 in Game 1 of the ALDS, his teammates were waiting to mob him at home plate. (GETTY IMAGES)

Jim Thome was all smiles after he hit a two-run homer against the Seattle Mariners during Game 5 of the ALCS.

The Indians could not contain themselves after they defeated the Seattle Mariners in Game 6 of the ALCS to clinch their first World Series berth since 1954.

Orel Hershiser and Dennis Martinez kept it light during batting practice before Hershiser's start in Game 1 of the World Series.

Cleveland-area high school students held the flag during opening ceremonies for Game 4 of the World Series at Jacobs Field.

The Indians were feeling good after they took care of the Atlanta Braves 7–6 in front of a home crowd in Game 3 of the World Series. (GETTY IMAGES)

Shortstop Carlos Baerga goes airborne in Game 6 of the World Series. (GETTY IMAGES)

Even though they lost, thousands of Indians fans gathered in downtown Cleveland on October 30 to thank their team for the wild ride and to wish them luck in '96.

In 1995, Jacobs Field played host to the first Indians playoff action in Cleveland in 41 years.

10

"Take Care of This Now or You're Probably Never Going to Play Baseball Again"

SANDY ALOMAR JR. WAS NOT supposed to play baseball in 1995. Doctors expected him to tend to his left knee throughout the summer. A little bit of agility work in the pool. A gradual return to walking and running. A lot of rest.

For the Indians, Alomar's absence was critical, given that he captured American League Rookie of the Year honors in 1990 and he was voted in as the starting catcher for the AL All-Star team in 1990, '91, and '92. He was the first rookie catcher to ever start the annual summer exhibition, and he earned his only Gold Glove Award later that year. By 1995, he had developed into a steady, veteran presence behind the plate and in the clubhouse.

But injuries had long been a concern by that point. In 1991, he was limited to 51 games. He limped into the All-Star break with a .241 batting average and a .592 OPS, and even those numbers were aided by a four-hit performance on the final Sunday of the first half. Alomar considered skipping the Midsummer Classic, feeling as though there were other candidates more worthy of making the trip to Toronto, but his teammates urged him to attend to appeal to the fans who checked his name on their ballots. He batted eighth for the AL, one spot ahead of his younger brother, Roberto, at that time the Blue Jays' second baseman.

Alomar's 1991 season ended in late July, and the injuries kept mounting. After he appeared in 51 games that year, he appeared in 89 games in 1992. Sixty-four games in 1993. Eighty games in 1994. Eventually, his knees begged for mercy. Toward the end of the strike-shortened season in 1994, Alomar's left knee regularly swelled. On August 9, the Indians' penultimate game before the players' strike commenced, the inflammation forced Alomar from action after the fifth inning. He sat out the next day. Doctors eventually cleaned out the area, but the pain persisted. Then he tore his meniscus during a winter league game in Puerto Rico that November, which required arthroscopic surgery.

"He had back surgery, knee surgeries," Carlos Baerga said. "I remember he came off the injured list for his back and the first day that he came back, he broke his finger. It was amazing. Blocking a ball. He went back on the injured list for two more months. He had bad luck. But every time he was healthy, he put up numbers."

There were instances in which Alomar would finish a game and then need fluid extracted from his knee or else the swelling would prevent him from squatting. When he arrived at spring training in Winter Haven, Florida, in 1995, Alomar felt a burning sensation in his left knee, different from anything he had previously experienced. He had atrophy in his muscles and he struggled to push through warmups. The Indians sent him to Dr. Richard Steadman in Colorado, where it was revealed that Alomar had a fracture in his plateau, near where the shin bone meets the knee. The injury would necessitate micro-fracture surgery, an uncommon and unfamiliar procedure at the time, and one that constituted a lengthy rehab process.

"He point-blank said, 'Hey, take care of this now or you're probably never going to play baseball again,'" Alomar said. "It could have been a career-ending injury. I was kind of freaking out."

Steadman sketched out an eight-month recovery plan, though Indians strength coach Fernando Montes aimed to carve that estimate in half. Alomar spent the first month in the pool, since he was unable to place any weight on his knee. He ultimately returned at the end of June, "a little ahead of time."

Yeah, just a little.

"I was never the same guy that I was in the minor leagues or my first couple years," Alomar said, "because I had to learn new muscle memories, how to hit, how to throw. It affected a lot of my—not fundamentals, but it affected my muscle memory, how I used to catch. I had to learn something new.

"I did my best to get over that hump and figure out a way to continue playing. When people have micro-fracture surgery now, people have a better idea. There's more technology now. They tend to keep you out almost a year. A lot of people don't come back from that, but thanks to the knee saver, I ended up playing all of those years after that."

Alomar avoided the injury bug during his ascent through the Padres' minor-league system. He developed a sense of invincibility, that he could log every inning behind the plate without enduring the customary aches and pains that nearly every catcher inherits. Only once did his body suffer. Following a home-plate collision at the end of the 1988 season, when he was playing at Triple-A, Alomar needed surgery. But that year, he and Gary Sheffield shared Minor League Player of the Year honors. In 1989, Alomar garnered the distinction again.

"He was an All-Star player," Baerga said. "Everybody talked about him all the time. And then when he got traded here, he became a star."

The final surgery score read six to three in the battle between left and right knee, respectively. His left knee is now mostly bone on bone, but Alomar took up cycling after his playing career to keep his legs in shape. He still wound up playing until 2007, a 20-year career that lasted beyond his 41st birthday. He never wanted to walk away from the sport as long as he could, well, actually walk.

"I felt like if I had something in the tank," Alomar said, "I could survive and be able to perform at this level."

Mike Hargrove played with Alomar's dad while with the Texas Rangers in 1977 and '78. He can recall the two boys, Sandy and Roberto, a couple of rugrats chasing each other through the clubhouse. Hargrove first noticed Alomar's playing potential when Alomar played at the Triple-A level in Las Vegas in 1988.

"It was real obvious that Sandy was far and away the best catcher in that league, physically and playing the game," Hargrove said. "He struggled that year early on, but Sandy had the physical tools to be a star player in the game for a long time.

"You see guys' physical attributes and you try to project those. There are certain things you look at that stand out. Sandy had good, soft hands and good mechanics. He was good behind the plate. For a very tall guy, he handled himself really well. He had a big arm. He had a sweet, quick stroke and he drove the ball. Everything screamed that Sandy would be a star player in the big leagues and you thought as long as he stayed healthy, he could play for a long time."

Alomar was an athlete from the beginning. While his brother fixated on baseball and basketball, Alomar tried his hand—err, hands—at tae kwon do and volleyball. He rode dirt bikes and motorcycles and dune buggies with his buddies.

"I knew deep down in my heart, I was just a baseball player," Alomar said, "but I wanted to interact with my friends."

Sandy Sr. owned a gas station, so Alomar washed cars and changed oil and flat tires to earn some extra money. He also delivered newspapers at 6:00 AM before he headed to school, and he wandered the busiest streets of Salinas in search of shoe-shining customers. Through those entrepreneurial endeavors, Alomar stockpiled enough cash to afford his own dirt bike. Sandy Sr. was not thrilled about his son's purchase, but he appreciated the teenager's initiative.

When Alomar reached the age of 15, he narrowed his focus to baseball. A league full of 20-year-olds needed a catcher, and Alomar aced his tryout, despite the age gap. A couple years later, he signed his first professional contract with the Padres.

Alomar was blocked in San Diego, though. The Padres already had Benito Santiago—another All-Star and Rookie of the Year Award recipient—to handle their catching duties. Alomar earned September promotions in 1988 and '89, but he knew he was on borrowed time in the Padres' organization. In December 1989, the Indians acquired both Alomar and Baerga in a trade that sent Joe Carter to San Diego and signaled the start of the Indians' roster overhaul and rebuilding project. Alomar became the Indians' primary catcher in 1990. Hargrove became his manager a year later.

By the time Alomar returned from his injury in 1995, the Indians were a force. He settled into the No. 9 spot in Hargrove's batting order and he sizzled at the plate, batting .385 with a 1.076 OPS for the first month. He ended the season with a .300 average and 10 home runs in 203 at-bats. Not bad for a guy who was never supposed to step foot in the batter's box that year.

"For me, the thing that really stands out with Sandy is his consistency," Hargrove said. "You knew pretty much what you were going to get, within certain parameters, out of Sandy every day. Sometimes it was the low end, sometimes it was the high end, but he was consistent as ever. He was consistent in his workouts, his work, his attitude. Everything was very consistent and anytime you see players who exhibit that sort of consistency, at least for me, those are the guys you really need to keep around, because they're the glue that holds the whole thing together."

He certainly earned the respect of his peers. When Paul Shuey made his Jacobs Field debut—his second major league appearance— in 1994, Alomar was his battery mate behind the plate. Alomar called for a fastball, but Shuey shook him off, requesting that the catcher flash a different number of fingers. Alomar, though, again called for a fastball. Shuey shook him off and stepped away from the pitching rubber. Ultimately, Shuey threw a curveball.

When the players retreated to the dugout after the inning, tensions escalated.

"We tried to kill each other," Shuey said. "But it was one of those things—I think it was the very best thing that could have happened. I had so much respect for him because he was sure that he had the right pitch. And I think I got some respect from him that I was willing to back it up. 'Hey, it's me. It's going to be my name in the paper the next day.' That's what I told him. From that day on, I just felt super comfortable with him back behind the dish."

Alomar developed into a leader in the clubhouse and on the field, a necessary calming presence among a roster full of larger-than-life personalities. Terry Francona invited Alomar to his coaching staff for that reason. Francona edged out Alomar for the managerial position after the 2012 season, and he praised Alomar for having no ego.

Hargrove: "Sandy wasn't necessarily a really vocal leader. Sandy just worked hard and expected everybody else to work hard with him. Sandy wasn't afraid to say something to somebody. Sandy was one of the leaders on the club."

Omar Vizquel: "He was really intense. He was one of the guys who never liked to lose."

Baerga: "Sandy showed everybody the kind of caliber he was as a catcher, being a leader and then as a hitter. He always came through in the special moments."

Vizquel: "What stands out about Sandy is how smart he is and the way he thinks. He sees the game different than everybody because he was a catcher."

Baerga: "I always looked up to Sandy, the way he played, the way he cared. He would show up on the field every day. He was a leader of our pitching staff, a guy who liked to study the game. He was an unbelievable leader."

Kenny Lofton: "He's meant a lot. Sandy was here from when we started this whole process and he's *still* here. Sandy was here when we started. He came over from San Diego. He was here in '90. He was here before any of us from that era and he's still here. For him to be in Cleveland this long, it's cool."

Vizquel: "He brought a lot of joy to this town. Sandy was one of the original people to build up the team. Him, Carlos Baerga, Kenny Lofton, Albert Belle—the guys who were in the organization from the beginning. They had to do it at the old ballpark and make the adjustment to the new one. It's great to see him still with the Indians. That's one of the greatest achievements, I think."

Hargrove: "I think Sandy, rightfully so, is a really integral part of the fabric of the Indians."

11

"It Was Poetic Justice"

Kenny Lofton never hesitated as he rounded third base, but when Mariners catcher Dan Wilson failed to demonstrate any sense of urgency while he retrieved the baseball, the Indians' speedster shifted into a higher gear. Ruben Amaro scored first. Few even remember that part of the equation, since Lofton came whipping around the corner like a neighborhood kid who just secured his driver's license. The Indians could sense it as they started to spill out of the dugout, with those World Series dreams starting to trickle into their brain space.

BUT LET'S BACK UP for a second. We'll get there, to perhaps the most momentous few seconds of the Indians' season, the brief period that converted the team's nervous energy and cautious optimism into pure elation.

The Indians were sitting on the tarmac in Boston following their sweep of the Red Sox in the Division Series when general manager John Hart started to wonder where the club would head next. At that moment, the Yankees gripped a 2–1 advantage in their series against the Mariners. Once that series reached its conclusion, the Indians would travel to either New York or Seattle. The teams finished with nearly identical records in the regular season, but many in the Indians' organization preferred to play the Yankees because they lacked a certain weapon that stood 82 inches tall.

Randy Johnson was the best pitcher in the American League. No one needed to tell that to the Indians, who watched him nearly spoil the grand opening of Jacobs Field a year earlier with his pursuit of the sport's most inconsiderate no-hitter. Johnson captured the Cy Young Award in 1995, the first of his five pieces of hardware. He also finished second in the balloting on three occasions.

In 1995, Johnson amassed an 18–2 record and a 2.48 ERA and he racked up 12.3 strikeouts per nine innings, but one statistic painted the full portrait. When Johnson pitched during the regular season, the Mariners posted a 27–3 record. Send the lanky lefty to the mound, scribble another tally in the win column.

The Mariners emerged triumphant in each of Johnson's final 10 starts, the stretch in which they loosened the Angels' stranglehold on the top spot in the division. In that span, Johnson logged a 1.45 ERA. And when California and Seattle squared off in a one-game playoff to determine the AL West champion, Johnson authored a complete-game three-hitter. He limited the Angels to one run and he struck out 12 batters. And he did all of that on three days of rest. So yeah, anyone could see why the Indians would prefer to face the team that couldn't trot out the otherworldly southpaw to the mound.

But because Johnson pitched in Game 163, he was unavailable until Game 3 of the ALDS against the Yankees, when he helped Seattle stave off elimination. The Mariners forced a decisive Game 5, which proceeded into extra innings, thanks to Seattle's eighth-inning rally. And who jogged in from the bullpen in the ninth, two days after he tossed 117 pitches? That fastball-flinging, slider-slinging guy nicknamed "The Big Unit." Johnson escaped a jam Norm Charlton had created in the ninth and struck out the Yankees in order in the 10th. New York scratched across a run in the 11th on a walk, a sacrifice bunt, and a Randy Velarde single, but Edgar Martínez delivered a two-run double off Jack McDowell (whose next pitch would come as a member of the Indians the following year) to send Seattle to the ALCS.

In the Pacific Northwest, fans referred to the team as the Miracle Mariners, or the Refuse to Lose Mariners. The franchise had existed for nearly two decades, but this was its first taste of the postseason. And when the Mariners hosted the Indians for the first two games of the ALCS, it did not take long for Cleveland's players to notice how starved the fan base was for a winner. Johnson joked that the city was known for Starbucks, grunge, and Microsoft, but he wondered if now it would be known for baseball, too.

The Kingdome was loud enough as it was, with every muttered word echoing off the roof or the walls of the building. But now with a hyped-up crowd? Charles Nagy said he could not hear himself think. Radio broadcaster Tom Hamilton joked that he felt like the Christians in the Roman Colosseum, and that he could not hear his partner on the mic, Herb Score, even though the two sat about a foot away from each other.

Lofton said it was the scariest and loudest place he ever played. He also was the one to silence that raucous audience, though. Or, at least, he was responsible for transforming the deafening cheers into anxious groans.

As Lofton rounded third base, he preyed on Wilson's casual retrieval of the baseball and Johnson's nonchalance in covering home plate. He knew he could score with a straight sprint down the line...

But we'll get to that.

The Indians were expected to reach this point, given their regular season dominance and their quick work of the Red Sox in the Division Series. The Mariners had been playing must-win games since mid-August. They were running on fumes, especially their pitching staff. The frantic ALDS finish left the Mariners scrambling a bit. Johnson would not be ready to pitch until Game 3. Lou Piniella's other options were either uninspiring or lacking full rest.

Enter Bob Wolcott, a month removed from turning 22 years old, with seven big-league appearances to his name. The Mariners were desperate. Wolcott was a second-round pick in the 1992 amateur draft. He had performed well in the minor leagues, but this was quite the leap. The Indians had some video they could study and some scouting reports they could pore over, but their intel was limited. Then again, did it matter?

Wolcott finished his career with 66 outings (58 starts), a 5.86 ERA, and 391 hits allowed in 325⅔ innings. In his career, opponents batted .299 with an .888 OPS against him. Wolcott ultimately bounced to the Diamondbacks and Red Sox, pitched for the Osaka Kintetsu Buffaloes in the Japan League in 2000, and briefly joined the Athletics in 2001. And that was a wrap on his professional career.

But on October 10, 1995, Wolcott was a well-regarded prospect taking the hill against the league's most daunting lineup in an effort to inch the Mariners closer to their first World Series appearance.

Here is how his night began:

Kenny Lofton: walk

Omar Vizquel: walk

Carlos Baerga: walk

He made 13 pitches to those three hitters. Only one weaved its way into the strike zone. Think he was a bit nervous? The Mariners already had a pair of relievers warming up in the bullpen and Piniella paid him a visit. The message (or, at least, the clean version) was this: just throw the ball over the plate and you might have a chance at giving us five or six innings because this current method certainly is not going to lead to that.

Imagine standing atop the mound, before 57,065 fans who were growing terribly impatient and skeptical, while Albert Belle, the most fearsome hitter on the planet, strolled to the plate with the bases loaded and no outs. There might not be a lonelier feeling in the world.

Wolcott struck him out. He said he liked how far Belle stood from the plate, that it gave him a wider area with which to work. Sure, rookie, whatever works for you against the guy who tormented opposing pitchers to the tune of 103 extra-base hits in only 143 games.

Then Wolcott induced a pop-out off the bat of Eddie Murray. One first-ballot Hall of Famer retired. And he got Jim Thome to ground out to second base. Another first-ballot Hall of Famer retired. No harm done. Miracle Mariners indeed. Belle thought the Indians let Wolcott off the hook, that they didn't exhibit enough patience at the plate to force him to find the strike zone with consistency. Belle spotted no evidence that suggested Wolcott wouldn't have continued to issue free passes. Instead, the Indians stranded three in the first inning and provided fuel for an already jazzed crowd.

That reversal of fortunes seemed to open some eyes in both dugouts. The Indians were salivating at the thought of an easy Game 1 win against an overmatched rookie. But he escaped what looked destined to develop into a disaster, and he wasn't done. Wolcott proceeded to fluster the Indians for seven innings. They stranded a couple of runners in the second, and Paul Sorrento grounded into a double play with the bases loaded in the third. Belle tied the game at 2–2 in the seventh with a solo home run, but the Mariners responded with a Luis Sojo RBI double in the bottom of the frame for the game's final run. In all, the Indians left 12 runners on base, and Piniella looked like a genius for tabbing Wolcott for the start, as the young righty scattered eight hits over seven surprisingly strong innings.

"The funny thing is," pitching coach Mark Wiley said, "most of the teams we played, most of the guys we had trouble with, it was either soft throwers who changed speeds or guys we didn't know. We were terrible—if they called a minor-league guy up, we would lose the game. It was unbelievable. We couldn't hit him. I don't know if it was familiarity or what, but we just didn't do it. We had to face Wolcott, and he opened it up and he beat us 3–2 in our first game in the ALCS and we didn't even know him and he was throwing, like, 79 mph. It was unbelievable."

The Indians won Game 2 without trouble, as Orel Hershiser delivered eight masterful innings and Carlos Baerga and Manny Ramirez carried the offense to a 5–2 victory.

Everything was setting the stage for a critical, late-series sequence, with Johnson's fastball caroming off Wilson's glove and rolling past the visitors' on-deck circle and toward the backstop, Amaro leisurely strolling to the plate and Lofton rumbling behind...

Wait, wait. Not yet.

First, Johnson started Game 3 in Cleveland with the series tied.

Herbert Perry and Alvaro Espinoza replaced lefties Thome and Sorrento in the starting lineup. Johnson retired the first nine batters he faced, but Lofton tripled to start the fourth and scored on Vizquel's sacrifice fly. In the eighth, Espinoza reached on an error, and Wayne Kirby pinch-ran and scored on Lofton's single. Lofton accounted for half of the Indians' four hits against Johnson, and he contributed to the scoring of both runs.

Johnson was not so much the problem in Game 3—Charlton was. The Mariners scooped up Charlton off the scrap heap in mid-July, following his early-season struggles in Philadelphia. Charlton posted a 1.51 ERA in 47⅔ innings with Seattle, with 11 strikeouts per nine innings and an opponent slash line of .143/.223/.199. Quite the find.

He silenced the Indians' bats in the ninth, 10th, and 11th, awarding his offense enough time to generate a rally. Jay Buhner struck in the top of the 11th, powering a three-run blast off Eric Plunk to the seats in right field. The Mariners had a 2–1 series lead.

The Indians sprinted out to a sizable lead in Game 4—following a ceremonial first pitch tossed by an impersonator of Charlie Sheen's "Wild Thing" Rick Vaughn character from *Major League*—with three runs in the first, another in the second, and two more in the third, all without Belle, sidelined with a sprained ankle, and Alomar, shelved with a stiff neck.

And now, it's time for the part of the script that reads more like fiction than non-fiction. Carlos Baerga opened the bottom of the fifth with a single to left field off Bob Wells. At the same time, a bright pink creature hobbled along the warning track in right-center. Slider, the Indians' furry, fuchsia mascot of some unidentified species, entered the open bullpen door and immediately dropped to the ground, writhing in pain in the bullpen dirt.

"The umpires don't see it. Slider is on the field," Bob Costas proclaimed on the national telecast. "The mascot fell out of the stands and he is hobbling toward the bullpen."

It had been a rainy day in Cleveland and the top of the wall was slick. Slider, the Indians' mascot since 1990, fell victim to the conditions as it wrapped up a between-inning performance with a somersault on the ledge between the seating bowl and the field. Slider never had a chance to use its hot dog slingshot, as it plummeted onto the field, landing on its right leg and suffering a knee dislocation and several torn ligaments. Well, the person in the costume, not the actual tubby critter. Before Slider could stagger over to the bullpen—where Indians reliever Julian Tavarez served as a pseudo paramedic—Baerga lined Wells' second pitch of the inning to left field, which prompted

Costas to wonder what might have happened had Baerga's base hit instead traveled to right-center, forcing a couple of Mariners outfielders to converge on a baseball hidden under one of Slider's flaps of pink fur.

"When you try to cry for help, that giant head kind of muffles the sound," Costas said. "You don't get the greatest projection when you're wearing a mascot head."

Slider arrived at Jacobs Field the next day with a pair of crutches and some bandages and received a standing ovation. Slider, by the way, was elected to the Mascot Hall of Fame in 2008, the fourth Major League Baseball mascot to earn induction.

"So first they lose Albert Belle with a sprained ankle," Costas said. "Now Slider goes down."

Just to add to the oddity: Slider was not the only wounded mascot involved in the series. During the ALDS, the Mariner Moose, donning inline skates, broke its ankle after crashing into the outfield wall in Seattle while being pulled by an ATV. Typical mascot shenanigans.

In order for Lofton to ace his moment in the spotlight—planting his left big toe on home plate just as Johnson realized there was a second steam engine bustling down the third base line—the Indians needed to secure the series lead before they returned to Seattle.

To do that, the Indians had to win Game 5 in their home ballpark.

The Indians trailed 2–1 in the sixth inning. The last thing they wanted to do was fly across the country, needing to win twice in the Pacific Northwest, with Johnson slated to start Game 6. Thome had tallied only five hits in 26 postseason at-bats when he approached the plate with Murray, the potential tying run, standing on second base. Chris Bosio misfired with his first two pitches to Thome. He misfired with the third as well, since Thome launched it into the second deck in right field for a go-ahead, two-run homer. Piniella stood motionless in the dugout, his mouth slightly agape, a stoic expression on his face, as if he was sitting through the worst stand-up comedy routine ever performed. The instant Thome crossed home plate, Piniella power walked to the mound to make a pitching change. As soon as Thome followed through on his swing, he tossed his bat away—one of the founding fathers of the modern bat flip, perhaps?—and pumped his right fist.

So the Indians simply needed one win in Seattle. And that was a nice luxury, considering Johnson was on the hill for the Mariners. The Indians scratched across an unearned run in the fifth, as Alvaro Espinoza reached on an error and scored on Lofton's single to left. Hargrove noted that Lofton was not exactly eager to face Johnson, but he proved quite valuable in leading off and disrupting the opposing pitcher's rhythm with his speed. Hargrove usually benched Thome and Sorrento against Johnson, but Lofton, also a left-handed hitter, typically remained atop the lineup. Hamilton called Lofton the top competitor the Indians ever employed, and Belle commended Lofton for pushing the envelope against the southpaw. Lofton carried the Indians' lineup in the ALCS, to the tune of a .458/.517/.625 slash line, with 11 hits, four walks, and five stolen bases in the six-game series.

Dennis Martínez protected that 1–0 advantage, as the 41-year-old—he kept thinking about how that number also represented the franchise's World Series drought, in years—delivered seven scoreless innings. Martínez joked that the odds were "200-to-1" that he could out-pitch Johnson. Perhaps he should have taken a detour to the Caesars Palace sports book in Las Vegas on his way to Seattle.

Tony Peña started the eighth with a double. Amaro replaced him at second base and advanced to third as Lofton placed a bunt single to the left of the mound. Lofton then swiped second base on the first pitch of the ensuing at-bat. Two pitches later, Johnson's fastball skipped off Wilson's glove and caromed to the wall just outside the visitors' dugout. Amaro trotted to the plate with ease, Vizquel waving him home while backpedaling out of the way. Lofton rounded third and pressed turbo, scampering to the plate and surprising Wilson, Johnson, and just about everyone else tuning in to the game.

Johnson stood upright, relaxed but ill-equipped to cover home plate until it was too late. Wilson scooped up the baseball, but was too lackadaisical to act quickly enough once Lofton made up his mind to bolt home. On a simple passed ball, the Indians scored twice, their narrow 1–0 edge ballooning into a seemingly insurmountable three-run advantage.

"I think it just showcased my aggressiveness, my speed," Lofton said. "I used it and we were very aggressive and we weren't afraid of anything. We weren't afraid of doing anything. I think that right there showed how aggressive we were throughout. We didn't take anything for granted."

Once Lofton bounced to his feet, he turned around to ensure that home plate umpire Drew Coble ruled him safe, and then he finished his 360 spin, shouting and skipping toward the dugout, where he slapped hands with Baerga, Amaro, and Kirby before he was swallowed whole by a swarm of teammates who smacked his helmet.

Hart referred to it as a moment that is frozen in time, a spectacle that showcased Lofton's fearlessness. Hargrove was stunned that Lofton even attempted such a daring endeavor, and he said he felt the blood rush to his fingertips. Lofton credited the play to his refusal to take anything for granted and his aggressive style of play, which had him constantly running hard out of the batter's box or striving to advance an extra base, anything to make the defense uncomfortable.

"You always advance with an aggressive turn just in case the guy bobbles it," Lofton said. "Sometimes guys kick a ball or something, you never know. But if you're lolly-gagging just to advance to one base, you can never advance that way. Once I looked up and Randy had his back turned and Dan Wilson was moping with his head down, I was like, 'Oh, shoot.' I just kept going. It's just instincts, reaction."

Nagy, in the dugout charting pitches at the time, said the team knew at that moment that it was headed to the World Series. Baerga tacked on a solo home run to make the final score 4–0, and after Jose Mesa retired the side in the ninth, the Indians congregated on the infield to celebrate the club's first trip to the doorstep of a championship since 1954.

"I can see it in my mind like it was yesterday, Kenny Lofton dashing home from second base in the Kingdome," Hamilton said. "You knew then that they were going to win the World Series. First off, nobody scores from second on a passed ball. To do it against Randy Johnson—he didn't like Kenny Lofton anyway, and Kenny didn't like Randy Johnson—it was poetic justice. You remember those kinds of moments."

12

"They Don't Make Them Like Jim Thome"

JIM THOME SCANNED THE ROOM and asked if anyone had heard Sean Casey's Chicago bar story. Before Casey even started to set the scene, Thome hunched over in his chair, laughing.

Casey took a deep breath.

It's 2004, we're [the Reds] playing the Cubs and every year, they just boat-race us. They just hit bombs. [Sammy] Sosa, all those guys are crushing us. On the corner, they have that one bar and all the fans come out and are like, 'You suck! You suck!' At the end of the year, there are seven games to go and we're playing four games in Chicago. I'm like, 'Fellas, our season's over. If we could take it to the Cubs and knock them out of the postseason, that would be our postseason.' First game, we get boat-raced [12–5]. We rattle off three [wins] against the Cubs, slap 'em around. Boom, turns out, mathematically, they're out of the postseason. So, here we go. Three games to go. We're going back to Cincy for three. It's travel day, so everyone has their suits on. A couple pops on the bus. We get to the corner and look out and everyone's depressed. No one's looking at the bus. We're fired up. We're in 5 o'clock traffic after a Thursday day game. So we're putting along, putting along, putting along. We get about eight blocks from Wrigley and I look over and there's a local bar, a packed house, but they're so depressed. And I'm like, 'We finally beat the Cubs.' I go to the bus driver and I'm like, 'Let me out.' The guy said, 'What? We're in traffic.' I said, 'I don't give a shit. Let me out.' In a full suit, I go into the bar and I yell, 'Hey, all you Cubs fans! The Cincinnati Reds just kicked your ass! Like they say in Chicago, better luck next season!' I thought this was a good idea until I see everyone go, like, 'We're gonna kill this guy!' People start running at me. I'm like, 'Jesus!' I run as fast as I can and I'm like, 'Open the door to the bus!' People are just pounding on the bus. I'm sitting next to [Barry] Larkin. I'm sweating. He goes, 'God damn, Casey, I've been in the big leagues for 19 years. I've seen a lot of things. That's the greatest thing I've ever seen.'"

The room—a cavernous conference room in a downtown Cleveland hotel during the week of the 2019 All-Star Game—was full of Thome's former teammates and coaches, and everyone erupted in laughter. Thome and Casey have maintained a friendship for decades, even though they only played together for a few weeks. The Indians selected Casey in the second round of the 1995 amateur draft. Was he thrilled to stand a chance at joining a powerhouse lineup, at learning from a slew of the sport's premier sluggers?

Not exactly.

"I was thinking, 'No, I'm in trouble,'" Casey said. "'I'm in trouble, because they have Jim Thome there.' When I got called up in '97, I was thinking, 'I'm gonna be out of here soon.' And I was."

Before the Indians jettisoned Casey to Cincinnati in exchange for starting pitcher Dave Burba in late March 1998, Casey and Thome developed a tight bond. Casey attended the Indians' first winter development program along with fellow prospects Danny Graves, Bartolo Colon, Enrique Wilson, and Bruce Aven. They toured Jacobs Field, listened to guest speakers, and worked out with team strength coach Fernando Montes. Thome lived in the Cleveland area, so he was hitting in the cages one day during the program.

"I remember literally being in awe," Casey said, "like, 'Oh, my God, it's Jim Thome. That's freaking awesome.' I remember going up to him and talking to him about hitting. I remember how nice of a person he was. It really impacted me, like, 'Wow, this is a really, really nice guy. He doesn't know me from Adam and he's taking the time to talk to me.'"

The Indians promoted Casey and Sexson to the major league roster for the first time in mid-September 1997. They joined the club in Chicago and accompanied them to Baltimore, the next stop on their road trip. As Casey boarded the charter, Thome grabbed him and said, "Hey, I want you to sit with me on the flight." Casey replied, "Are you serious?"

"No idiot rookie goes to the back of the plane unless you're invited by Jim Thome," Casey said.

Casey can recall Matt Williams—a former All-Star, Gold Glove winner, and home run champ—sitting in front of him. David Justice—an All-Star, Rookie of the Year Award winner, and World Series hero—sat to his right. Orel Hershiser, a former Cy Young Award winner, and Charles Nagy, an All-Star, sat nearby as well.

"And me, sitting back there," Casey said. "I'm so uncomfortable, feeling so out of place. But I was so excited. Thome said to come sit with him. What am I going to say, 'No?'"

But then veteran infielder Jeff Manto stood up and peered at Casey.

"Hey, rookie," Manto said, "what are you doing sitting in the back?"

Casey opened his mouth, but words refused to surface. Thome interjected.

"I told him to sit with me so we could chat a little bit," Thome said.

"That was really cool for me," Casey said. "Like, this guy is taking me under his wing. It was really, really cool. That whole time I was up in '97, Jim and I struck up a friendship. It's funny, because it felt like he had been in the big leagues for 10 years, but he broke in so young. At the time, he was 27 and I was 23."

Before the trade, Casey spent spring training with the Indians in 1998. Every morning at 8:00 AM, defensive coordinator Brian Graham would throw balls in the dirt for Casey, Thome, and Sexson to scoop at first base. Casey was enamored by Thome's glove, a Wilson brand piece of leather, perfectly broken in, black and tan with Thome's name on it.

Thome would go first. Then Sexson. Then Casey. But Thome would loan his glove to Casey for his turn, since he knew Casey loved the glove. When the Indians traded Casey on the final day of spring training, Thome visited his fellow first baseman as he cleaned out his locker.

"Hey, Case, take my glove with you and use it," Thome said.

Casey still owns the glove.

"That's who he is," Casey said. "We've kept a friendship since then. I remember Adam Dunn and Austin Kearns coming up to the big leagues. I tried to make them feel like, 'Hey, you're not a peon. You're a big-league player and we're all human beings here.' Not that the rookies don't have to do their rookie stuff, but as far as the human dignity and respect for another person goes, the way Jim treated me was big on me doing the same thing, paying it forward to other guys who came up, making them feel comfortable. That's the biggest thing when you get to the big leagues.

"Jim is just a rare breed. They don't make them like Jim Thome. Not even anymore—they don't make them like Jim Thome. The guy is one of the greatest baseball players of all time, with the home runs that he's hit. If you hung out with him for four days, you would never know who he is. You go on a hunting trip with him and talk to him and you may never know who he is. He's such an unbelievable person."

That's the resounding sentiment from those who played with Thome in the early '90s, when he was a toothpick-skinny third baseman, and those who marveled at his mere presence in the clubhouse 20-some years later, when he was a sturdy designated hitter. The common threads along that metamorphosis? Home runs and human decency.

"I was blessed to play at a young age and got the chance to do it when I was a baby," Thome said. "Looking back, it's so cool to watch that progression."

No one knew Thome would evolve into a first-ballot Hall of Famer, or that a statue depicting his batting stance—oft-mimicked by daydreaming kids in their backyards—would stand tall near the ballpark gates in the heart of downtown Cleveland. Or even that the Indians would one day retire his No. 25.

Well, that might be because when Thome socked the first of his 612 big-league home runs, he was wearing No. 6. The lanky 21-year-old lifted Steve Farr's 1–0 offering into the deserted upper deck in right field at Yankee Stadium on October 4, 1991, the third-to-last day of the regular season. The three-run shot vaulted the last-place Indians to a 4–2 win.

"The moment kind of stops, if that makes sense," Thome said. "The moment stops and you're like, 'Okay. I want to do that again.' That's what keeps you coming back."

The Indians knew he wielded power potential, but he needed plenty of refining. They selected him in the 13th round of the 1989 draft, a country bumpkin shortstop from Illinois Central College. Thome always hit for average in the minor leagues, but the power came and went.

Enter Charlie Manuel.

"He would never let you get too high or too low during the good and bad times," Thome said.

Manuel is responsible for that signature stance, in which Thome points his bat toward the sky before tucking it between his head and his back shoulder. The open stance put Thome's hips and hands in a better position to generate power.

"If you read books about hitting," Thome said, "one of the things that Ted Williams always talked about is hips and hands. When I was younger, I really had no hips. I was a locked-off hitter, kind of closed hips. Once Charlie moved me on the plate and opened me up, everything changed. Everything."

Thome and Manuel developed a close, long-lasting bond. Manuel rose from the minor-league ranks to serve as the Indians' hitting coach from 1994 to '99, before he replaced Mike Hargrove as manager. When Manuel would accompany Albert Belle to the batting cages in the mid-90s, Thome would ask to join them. The two still chat on the phone every few weeks. And when Thome was chosen to manage the American League squad in the 2019 Futures Game, he picked Manuel to occupy the role of team hitting coach. During batting practice that Sunday afternoon, Thome and Manuel leaned on the cage like old times and analyzed swing mechanics.

"Thome loves talking hitting," Casey said. "Whenever we talk hitting, Charlie's name will come up. 'Charlie said this.' 'Charlie said that.' I love talking hitting, some of the things he did, what his approach was, what he was thinking, all of that stuff. He and I will get dinner together, hang out. We're always talking hitting when we're hanging out. To talk hitting with a guy like Jimmy, I feel like I won the lottery or something."

The 1994 season was Thome's first full year in the big leagues, though the players' strike halted the Indians' progress. So the '95 campaign was when Thome truly showcased his potential. He hit for average (.314). He exhibited patience and a keen eye at the plate (97 walks and a .438 on-base percentage). He hit for power (25 home runs, 29 doubles, and a .558 slugging percentage). And that October, he hit several series-shifting homers. Opposing pitchers pitched around Albert Belle at their own peril, knowing Eddie Murray, Thome, and Manny Ramirez—perfectly capable hitters in their own right—lurked behind him.

Thome is the Indians' all-time home run leader, with 337 of his 612 homers coming while he donned a Cleveland uniform. He clubbed 190 of those homers at Progressive Field. Farr was merely his first victim; he ultimately tagged 403 different pitchers for a home run. He teed off against Roger Clemens eight times and against Justin Verlander on seven occasions. He conquered Rick Reed nine times, including seven times in 16 at-bats during the 2002 season, when Thome totaled a career-high and franchise-record 52 home runs.

Thome hit home runs *for* five different teams and *against* 30 different teams. He trotted around the bases at 38 different ballparks. He tallied 48 multi-homer games, including a pair of three-homer performances. He recorded his 610th and 611th home runs against the Indians. His final blast came against Blue Jays hurler Carlos Villanueva, 7,664 days after Thome's first career long ball. Villanueva was 7 years old when Thome hit his first far one off Farr at Yankee Stadium.

A few hours before the Futures Game, Thome delivered a pregame speech to the prospects about 30 years his junior. He shared with them how honored he was to have the opportunity to manage them for the day and how thrilled he was to watch them on the field.

"You look at the guys and they're like, 'Oh yeah, that's cool,'" Casey said. "I had to step in and remind them, 'If you could take a walk around this park, you're going to see a couple statues, and that guy is one of them—with 612 home runs, one of the greatest human beings to ever play the game.'"

But that's Thome.

"I almost feel like he's more humble now," Casey said. "He's always been humble. He's never changed. But when you're a player and you look back on your career, you're like, 'Yeah, I was really good.' Sometimes you think you're better than you were. Jim almost went the other way. You can hang out with Jimmy for five days and you would never know he was Jim Thome, one of the greatest players ever. He's just such a humble, nice guy. He never believed his press."

Thome endured a messy divorce with the Indians after the 2002 season. Following the departure of lineup staples such as Ramirez, Kenny Lofton, and Roberto and Sandy Alomar, Thome emerged as the face of the franchise, only to join the Phillies on a lucrative long-term contract after setting the Indians' home run record. He bounced around the league after that, heading to Chicago and Minnesota. And in 2011, after some initial hesitation, he returned to Cleveland in an August waiver deal with the Twins. He spent the final five weeks of the season with his original team.

At the time of the trade, Tribe pitcher Josh Tomlin asked the clubhouse attendants to order him a Thome jersey. Tomlin was a bit nervous, unsure if Thome, in his 21st major league season, would bother completing a favor for a second-year hurler. He pestered those in the organization who were familiar with Thome, asking them if they thought Thome would sign the jersey.

"Everyone who played with him or knew him was like, 'Go talk to the man and you'll understand why we're saying he'll sign it. He'll enjoy it. He won't shun you or anything. He'll sign it and he'll be happy to sign it,'" Tomlin said.

When Tomlin approached Thome about signing it at the end of the season, Thome was taken aback.

"He was like, 'Oh, are you serious? You really want me to?'" Tomlin said. "He didn't think he was any better or more special or more deserving than anybody else."

To Josh: You're a great teammate, a class act. I enjoyed playing with you. Best of luck to you in the future—Jim Thome, 600 HR Club

Throughout high school, Jason Kipnis pointed his bat toward center field, a la Thome, before he settled into his batting stance. Kipnis joined the Indians in late July 2011. One month later, he and Thome were teammates.

"When you come in your rookie year," Kipnis said, "you're already wide-eyed from the league itself and players around the league. Then you're talking to one of the guys you've emulated your swing after. He never let the success define who he is. He's a great storyteller, a good friend, a good person, a family man."

Thome spent the final days of his big-league career with the Orioles in 2012, and Zach McAllister, his former teammate in Cleveland, surrendered home run No. 611. Thome yanked a two-run shot to right in the seventh inning at Progressive Field on July 21, 2012. The homer provided Baltimore with a 2–1 advantage and spoiled McAllister's shutout bid. In Thome's previous at-bat, though, he nearly launched McAllister's first-pitch offering beyond the center-field wall. As Michael Brantley hauled in the fly ball, McAllister and Thome made eye contact and smiled.

"Like, 'I got away with it,'" McAllister said. "That was pretty cool to be able to do that against him, but he was able to get me the next at-bat."

Three innings later, Thome struck. The two both hail from Peoria, Illinois, and Thome has donated autographed memorabilia to McAllister's annual baseball camp. He also signed a photo of the two of them.

"At the time, I didn't want to smile about it," McAllister said, "but it's cool now. A Hall of Famer, he got me."

The Indians were playing in Detroit in 2018 on the afternoon of Thome's induction into the Baseball Hall of Fame. After their game, players sat at their lockers and listened to Thome's speech. Those who had played with him seven years earlier, and others who had interacted with him during his occasional visits to Cleveland, all heard precisely what they had anticipated. Moments before Thome started talking, reading a speech he had rehearsed over and over, even during a practice run in Cooperstown, Tomlin made a prediction: "He's just going to act like it's no big deal, like he doesn't belong there, when the truth is, he probably belongs in there a lot more as a human being than he does as a baseball player."

Only seven players tallied more home runs than Thome's 612: Barry Bonds, Hank Aaron, Babe Ruth, Alex Rodriguez, Willie Mays, Albert Pujols, and Ken Griffey Jr. And, incredibly, the guy who ranks eighth on the league's all-time home run list spent much of the 1995 pennant-winning season batting sixth or seventh in

Mike Hargrove's lineup. Still, he made his presence felt as often as any middle-of-the-order hitter did, especially when it counted most. Thome's two-run blast in the first inning in Game 3 of the ALDS essentially shut the door on the Red Sox in 1995. He hit a pair of key home runs late in the Indians' ALCS triumph against the Mariners. He authored a couple of critical hits—a go-ahead two-run single and what wound up being the game-saving home run—as the Indians staved off elimination in Game 5 of the World Series. Thome's 17 postseason home runs rank seventh all-time, though many of the players situated ahead of him on the list racked up far more plate appearances.

"I remember [Orel] Hershiser saying, 'You can't get every big hit,'" Thome said, "'but the hits that you get are meaningful. Don't try to be the hero every at-bat.'"

In 1995, Thome was a young, calming presence amid an oft-chaotic clubhouse. He was typically glued to Manuel's hip. The evening before the Futures Game in 2019, the coaching staffs of each side congregated on the sixth floor of the Westin hotel in downtown Cleveland. As the banter began, Thome walked in with a guitar in his hand.

"Hey, Omar," Carlos Baerga shouted to his former middle infield mate, Omar Vizquel, "now Thome's a guitar player! Thome, is that what Charlie taught you?"

Thome shook hands with his opposing manager, National League skipper Dennis Martínez, another former Cleveland teammate.

"Wait 'til you see my lineup," Thome told him.

The two coaching staffs filed into separate conference rooms to begin preparations for the next day's exhibition. Thome selected Casey, Manuel, Burba, Juan Nieves, Nick Punto, and Ever

Magallanes to his staff. Martínez, Baerga, Vizquel, Nagy, Alvaro
Espinoza, Jerry Manuel, and Ruben Niebla comprised the NL staff.
A rep from Major League Baseball revealed to the AL coaches that
the NL staff was guaranteeing a victory, to which Thome replied,
"They don't know what's ahead of them."

Naturally, the two sides wrapped up the evening in a 2–2 deadlock, so neither staff earned bragging rights. Thome snapped a
picture while sitting at Terry Francona's desk, occupying the role
of manager for the day. He sent Francona the photo, and when the
two bumped into each other a couple days later, Thome thanked
Francona for allowing him to use the office.

"Do you feel dumber?" Francona quipped. "Sit in that chair and
you feel dumber."

The afternoon following Thome's managerial debut, Thome
attended an MLB Network production meeting. He sat on a couch
with Pedro Martínez, Al Leiter, Casey, and Harold Reynolds, who
pointed out that hitting masterminds Thome, Casey, and Manuel
all shared a dugout the previous night for a team that was being
blanked until the game's final moments. Reynolds said he wished
he had been within shouting distance.

"Know how much trash we would have talked?" Reynolds said.

Reynolds mentioned the plaque beyond center field that marks
where Thome's ballpark-record 511-foot blast cratered in 1999. "The
wind blew it," Thome insisted. "I can't hit a ball that far."

The truth is, it was a hot, humid evening, with a temperature of
87 degrees and a 15-mph wind blowing out to center at first pitch
for the nightcap of the Indians' doubleheader against the Royals
on July 3, 1999. Thome can recall Manuel telling him, "Son, if
you hit one, they might talk about it forever." Thome hit one all

right. Once the baseball completed its orbit around the moon, it bounced onto the street beyond the ballpark gates. When Reynolds first asked where the ball landed, as the two were walking onto the field, Thome pointed toward the street.

"The one time Jim Thome was not Mr. Humble," Reynolds said, laughing, and pretending to place a telescope to his eye. "He was like, 'It was out there.'"

13

"We Just Thought This Was Our Moment"

IN THE '70S, JIM THOME would toss rocks in the air and take giant hacks in his yard. The little kid would set the scene with his own narration.

Seventh game of the World Series. Bases loaded. Thome at the plate.

It is not an uncommon practice, a child mentally transforming the backyard into a baseball diamond, a cluster of trees into the outfield fence, the chirping birds and scurrying squirrels into a stadium full of anxious, vocal fans. It's never the third inning of a Tuesday night game in May. It's always Game 7 of the World Series, the game, the season, the player's legacy all hanging in the balance.

But fast forward nearly 20 years. There was Thome, standing along the baseline at Fulton County Stadium in Atlanta, being recognized before a national TV audience on the grandest stage that the sport can provide. Any kid can dream it. Few can actually experience it.

"I'm being introduced as a 25-year-old kid going, 'God, this is like a dream come true. This is what you dream about. I'm 25 and I'm getting introduced in October in a World Series.' It's hard to put it into words," Thome said.

Everything had come full circle. Until Greg Maddux misfired with the first offering of the 1995 World Series, the previous World Series pitch had come two years earlier. In fact, that pitch ultimately disappeared beyond the left-field fence at the Skydome, as Joe Carter—yes, that Joe Carter—lived out a fantasy similar to the one Thome would conjure up in his mind. Carter, of course, indirectly launched the Indians' build toward 1995. The Indians traded him for prospects Sandy Alomar Jr. and Carlos Baerga (and Chris James) in 1989, as Cleveland's front office finally committed to a full-scale rebuild.

Four years later, with the Indians' assembly of young talent inching closer to legitimacy, Carter provided the Blue Jays with some World Series heroics. His three-run home run, against Phillies closer Mitch Williams—who was slipping to the dirt as he released the ball—clinched Toronto its second consecutive championship. With one out in the bottom of the ninth and a couple of Hall of Famers, Rickey Henderson and Paul Molitor, on base, Carter pounced on a 2–2 pitch and converted the Blue Jays' 6–5 deficit into an 8–6 triumph. Once the baseball sailed past the outfield wall, Carter leapt in the air three times along the first-base line. His helmet popped off of his head as he rounded the bag, his celebratory trot around the bases just beginning.

Much changed between that moment and the start of the next World Series, a mere 729 days later. The Indians evolved from a work-in-progress that played half its games in a mostly deserted cavern to a cocky bunch highlighted by a star-studded lineup that aimed to suck the life out of its opponents in its warm, inviting new ballpark.

In 1993, the 104-win Braves fell to the Phillies in six games in the National League Championship Series, even though Atlanta outscored Philadelphia 33–23. The Phillies eked out three one-run victories, including two in extra innings. The Phillies flustered an uncharacteristically erratic Maddux, who surrendered six runs (five earned) on six hits and four walks in 5⅔ innings. For the third consecutive October, a first-place Braves team ended its season on a sour note.

At the time of the strike in 1994, the Braves trailed the Expos by six games in the NL East standings. The Phillies had tumbled to fourth place, a punchless lineup failing to support a solid pitching staff. In '95, the Braves returned to the top of the division. They were always built on the foundation of a dominant starting rotation. In '93, Maddux, Tom Glavine, John Smoltz, and Steve Avery combined to log 973⅓ innings, with Avery's 223⅓ innings the lowest total among the four. Avery and Smoltz each made 35 starts. Maddux and Glavine made 36 apiece. Those four workhorses anchored the roster again two years later as Atlanta started another October journey. This time, though, the Braves had some young reinforcements in Bobby Cox's batting order.

The Braves owned home-field advantage for the 1995 World Series, in part because of the work stoppage the previous year. At that time, home-field advantage alternated between the American League and National League side each year. Typically, the AL club hosted the extra game in odd years, but the players' strike wiped out the 1994 postseason and reversed the customary pattern. So the Braves welcomed the Indians to Atlanta for Games 1 and 2 in 1995, even though the Indians finished the regular season with 10 more victories.

The two teams were polar opposites.

The Braves were no strangers to the postseason, having reached the World Series in 1991 and '92—falling short against the Minnesota Twins and Toronto Blue Jays, respectively—plus the letdown against the Phillies in the NLCS in '93. They did, however, have a handful of emerging key cogs in the lineup: rookie third baseman Chipper Jones (an eventual first-ballot Hall of Famer), catcher Javy Lopez, and left fielder Ryan Klesko.

The Indians, on the other hand, lacked postseason experience, aside from a handful of veterans. Orel Hershiser earned World Series MVP honors with the Los Angeles Dodgers in 1988, when he silenced Oakland's bats in Games 2 and 5. That postseason, Hershiser posted a 1.05 ERA, with a .439 opponent OPS, in six outings. He threw three complete games, including two in the World Series. In the decisive Game 5, Hershiser held Dave Henderson, Jose Canseco, Dave Parker, and Mark McGwire, the vaunted meat of the Athletics' lineup, hitless in 14 at-bats.

Eddie Murray had twice appeared in the World Series—in 1979 and in 1983—with the Baltimore Orioles. Dennis Martínez also played on that 1979 Baltimore team that dropped Game 7 at Memorial Stadium against the Willie Stargell–led Pittsburgh Pirates (the team backed by Sister Sledge's disco hit, "We Are Family"). Tony Peña batted .409 for the St. Louis Cardinals in the 1987 World Series. Dave Winfield did not receive any postseason playing time for the Indians in 1995, but he imparted wisdom on his teammates all year. His World Series experience included a trip with the New York Yankees in 1981 and another with the Blue Jays in 1992, when Toronto topped the Braves in six games.

Paul Sorrento played sparingly on the 1991 Twins team that knocked off Atlanta in the Fall Classic. Sorrento went 0–for–2 with two strikeouts in that seven-game heavyweight bout. He pinch-hit with two outs in the bottom of the ninth of Game 7, with the score knotted at 0–0 and runners on the corners, giving him a chance to etch his name into Minneapolis sports lore, a chance to eat free silver butter knife sirloins at Murray's Steakhouse for the rest of his life... but he struck out against Alejandro Peña.

And here he was again, staring down that same Braves rotation with the Commissioner's Trophy hanging in the balance.

"It was the Braves again," he said, "the same guys, the same cast of characters—except for Maddux. He wasn't there yet in '91."

No, Maddux joined the Braves in December 1992, shortly after he won his first Cy Young Award with the Cubs. So it was that same, stout Braves rotation... but better.

The 1995 matchup was a classic battle of strengths, a showcase of elite hitting against elite pitching, perhaps the greatest on-field example of the old "unstoppable force versus immovable object" paradox. The Indians led the AL in just about every hitting category imaginable. The Braves, meanwhile, had constructed a pitching factory. They led the NL in ERA (3.44), complete games (18), strikeouts, fewest hits allowed, fewest runs allowed, and fewest home runs allowed.

Maddux, Atlanta's Game 1 starter, was the captain of the rotation, the winner of four consecutive NL Cy Young Awards. He was the first pitcher in league history to win four straight pieces of hardware, until Randy Johnson matched his feat in 2002. In 1994 and 1995, Maddux's selections were unanimous, as he received all 28 first-place votes each year.

Maddux's numbers in 1994 and '95 are NSFW (not safe for work). Examine these in the privacy of your own home, and keep young children away.

1994: 16–6 record, 1.56 ERA, four home runs allowed and
31 walks in 202 innings
1995: 19–2 record, 1.63 ERA, eight home runs allowed and
23 walks in 209⅔ innings

He could paint the corners as well as any pitcher in the league, with precision command and just enough late movement to prevent hitters from squaring up the baseball and launching it into orbit. The Indians had unearthed a way to conquer Johnson in the ALCS; Maddux was at least Johnson's equivalent, if not an even taller order. (That's *taller* in a figurative sense, of course. Maddux was about 10 inches shorter than Johnson.)

On top of Maddux's otherworldly ability, the Braves' rotation boasted another pair of eventual Hall of Fame inductees in Glavine and Smoltz.

Glavine: 16–7, 3.08 ERA, only nine home runs allowed in 198⅔ innings

Smoltz: 12–7, 3.18 ERA, 193 strikeouts in 192⅔ innings

Atlanta's No. 2 and No. 3 starting pitchers would have been aces on just about any other staff. Southpaws Avery and Kent Mercker rounded out the Braves' starting rotation. Those five started all but three of the Braves' regular season games. Mark Wohlers, equipped with a killer fastball and a thriller of a mullet, typically silenced the opposition in the ninth inning. He tallied 90 strikeouts in 64⅔ innings during the regular season, and he surrendered only two home runs.

If any offensive attack could challenge the Braves' unparalleled pitching staff, it was the one that had Thome and Manny Ramirez, a pair of young stalwarts, batting sixth and seventh. At least, that was the prevailing thought entering the series.

The Indians had plenty of pitching, too. They led the AL in ERA, issued the fewest number of walks, and allowed the second-fewest amount of hits. And by the same token, the Braves' lineup was not to be overlooked. They ranked next-to-last in the NL with a .250 batting average, but they ranked second with 168 home runs. The lineup had some soft spots, but with talented young hitters such as Jones, Klesko, and Lopez and proficient experienced veterans in David Justice, Fred McGriff, and Marquis Grissom, it was not an easy nine for opposing pitchers to navigate.

When Justice joined the Indians in a 1997 trade, he told pitching coach Mark Wiley, "Mark, there are two things about Cleveland and Atlanta. I come over here to Cleveland and everybody appreciates the offense. Nobody talks about the pitching. It's the exact opposite [in Atlanta]. No matter how good you are as an offensive player in Atlanta, everybody just talks about the pitching."

This heavyweight bout was the perfect showcase for a league that had been reeling from a player's strike the previous year, which wiped out the postseason altogether. This was the first World Series in two years, and Thome wasn't the only one who had to pinch himself to prove it was real. Cleveland's fans had waited 41 years for the opportunity.

"It was unbelievable," Wiley said. "Everybody had Indians everything. It had been such a long drought and we had been selling out every game. To every fan, it was the biggest thing ever in Cleveland. It was crazy."

Game 1: The Release Point

Something had to give. Cleveland was hungry for a title. None of the city's major professional teams had achieved glory since the Browns captured the NFL championship with a 27–0 drubbing of the Baltimore Colts in December 1964. None of Atlanta's three major professional teams—the Braves, the Falcons, or the Hawks—had won a title. Period. And in Atlanta, there was a heightened sense of desperation, bordering on the brink of exasperation, given how close the Braves had come throughout the first half of the decade. Only one fan base would be able to soothe its sports-induced wounds, though.

What a start: Kenny Lofton manufactured a run in the first inning as he reached on an error by Rafael Belliard, the Braves' typically sure-handed shortstop. Lofton stole second and third and scored on a Carlos Baerga bouncer to short. Throughout the ALCS and World Series, Lofton ignited the Indians' offense. He swiped five bases in the ALCS against the Mariners and six more against the Braves.

Chin music...kind of: Hershiser served up a solo home run to McGriff to right field to open the second inning, which tied the score at 1–1. Sandy Alomar Jr. called for a fastball away, but Hershiser missed over the middle of the plate. McGriff socked 493 homers during his career, and 10 more during postseason play. If a pitcher made a mistake, he often pounced. In the ensuing at-bat, Hershiser threw a pitch up and in to Justice, who dropped his bat. Hershiser barked at him and applauded him for his theatrics. Hershiser did not think the pitch sailed uncomfortably close to him.

Send help: McGriff started the bottom of the seventh with a walk. Hershiser's full-count fastball missed the strike zone by three zip codes. Then Hershiser walked Justice on four pitches. Pitching coach Mark Wiley emerged from the dugout to see how Hershiser was feeling, since his pitch count had crept up to 101. Often a pitcher will scoff at the notion that he is tired and will assure the coach that he can escape whatever jam he has created. The coach will retreat to the dugout, cross his fingers, and watch the action unfold. But Hershiser—the guy nicknamed The Bulldog, who entered the start with a dazzling 7–0 record, 1.47 ERA, and .485 opponent OPS in his postseason career—told Wiley that he didn't have it, that he could not find his proper release point and that he needed to be replaced. That came as a surprise to Wiley. Hershiser was aiming to keep the ball away from the left-handed hitters, out of fear of surrendering a home run that they could yank to right field. But he kept the ball away from both the batters and the strike zone. Hershiser pitched the Indians to victory in Game 2 of the AL Division Series against the Red Sox. He was named the ALCS MVP for his sterling efforts against Seattle in Games 2 and 5. But after a strong start to Game 1 of the World Series, he exited in a hurry with the go-ahead runs on base.

The manager is usually the one to exercise a pitching change, not the pitching coach. Wiley, though, had no choice but to call for Paul Assenmacher. The veteran lefty walked pinch-hitter Mike Devereaux, who was simply trying to drop down a sacrifice bunt. That loaded the bases and prompted Mike Hargrove to summon Julian Tavarez from the bullpen. The Braves grabbed the lead when Luis Polonia hit a bouncer to Omar Vizquel, who bobbled the ball as he stepped on second base to record a force out. He never really had control of the baseball, which irked Atlanta manager Bobby Cox. A Belliard squeeze bunt scored another run.

Not enough: Lofton manufactured the Indians' second run, too. He singled in the ninth, advanced to third on a Vizquel groundout, and scored on an errant throw to third. Yeah, speed can be valuable. But then Baerga popped out to end the game.

Final: Braves 3, Indians 2

Game 2: Precious Cargo

They might be the five words a sportswriter least expects to hear.

No, not, "That article was a masterpiece," or "Your flight is on time," though those might tie for second. No, Dennis Martínez once uttered the one sentence that shocked three scribes riding in a Chevy Lumina.

"Can I have a ride?"

It's rare enough for a professional athlete to ask a media member for a ride, but Martínez was that night's starting pitcher. Oh, and it just so happened to be Game 2 of the 1995 World Series. Unfortunately for the trio of stunned sportswriters, Uber was about 15 years from its conception. The hotel shuttle was running late and Martínez needed to get to Atlanta Fulton-County Stadium. And this rental car full of gentlemen who already planned to chronicle his evening now determined his fate.

Bud Shaw was at the wheel and Paul Hoynes rode in the passenger's seat. Bill Livingston, who sat in the back with Martínez, told Shaw, "Keep us out of the headlines." Martínez chatted the entire drive, about the Indians' Game 1 loss, about the right-hander's triumph in Seattle in Game 6 of the ALCS. His start in Atlanta that night would mark his first World Series outing since the 1979 battle between his Baltimore Orioles and the Pittsburgh Pirates. In 1995, Martínez's 20th season in the big leagues, he went 12–5 with a 3.08 ERA. He earned his fourth career trip to the All-Star Game.

When they arrived at the ballpark—not at the media lot, but at the tunnel that weaved toward the visitors' locker room—a skeptical guard halted them in their tracks. They explained they were escorting the starting pitcher to his job site. Martínez looked at the guard and said, "Howdy." The guard relented.

Martínez pitched into the sixth inning, but Javy Lopez tagged him for a two-run homer and the Braves emerged with a 4–3 victory. The three writers crafted their stories late into the night. Martínez opted to join his teammates on the bus rather than wait around for another ride.

Senior citizens: Sixteen years elapsed between Martínez's first World Series trip and his last. That stretch between Fall Classic starts—a mere 5,854 days—marked the longest in MLB history. He took the ball in Game 2, and he received some early backing from another veteran on the roster in Murray, who became the third-oldest player to hit a home run in the World Series. Murray's two-run blast in the second inning off Glavine was his first hit from the right side of the plate in the playoffs.

Costly mistake: The Braves took a 4–2 lead after Lopez powered a two-run homer to dead center in the sixth. The Indians could have mounted a threat in the eighth, as Ramirez singled with one out. But with Thome at the plate, Lopez called for a two-strike fastball, popped to his feet, and fired a snap throw to first, where McGriff made a sweeping tag to erase Ramirez. It was a critical error by the 23-year-old, as Thome eventually walked. Peña dodged harm and, for the second consecutive game, Baerga popped out to the left side to end the game. Vizquel, the potential tying run, was stranded at second base.

Final: Braves 4, Indians 3

Game 3: Nothing More Fitting Than a Walk-Off

There were fireworks both before and after Game 3, the first World Series tilt in Cleveland in 41 years. NBC reporter Hannah Storm had set up an interview with Lofton, to take place in the home dugout after batting practice. That was news to Albert Belle, who had grown tired of the media mob infringing on the players' space. He unleashed a verbal tirade toward Storm. The league ultimately fined Belle $50,000 for his actions, which the Indians simply took out of his salary.

Home, sweet home: The Indians collected only eight hits in the first two games, which wasted decent pitching, and by the time they came to bat in the bottom of the first of Game 3—with a raucous crowd that had waited decades to attend a World Series contest—they already trailed 1–0. In 12 career postseason starts, Smoltz had posted a 2.40 ERA. In four career World Series starts, he had logged a 1.95 ERA. He didn't hang around for long in Game 3, though.

Lofton singled and scored—sans his helmet, which flew off as he approached third base—on Vizquel's triple to the right-field corner in the first. Vizquel scored on Baerga's groundout. For the third straight game, the Indians possessed an early advantage on the scoreboard. This time, they added to it.

An early departure: Lofton, ever the catalyst, opened the third inning with a double. Vizquel attempted to bunt him over to third, but he reached safely when the baseball refused to trickle foul, the Braves infielders doing everything in their might but huff and puff and blow the ball past the white chalk. Baerga and Albert Belle delivered RBI singles to pad the Indians' lead. Murray struck out, but Smoltz walked Thome and then retreated to the dugout as Ray Charles' tune "Hit the Road, Jack" blared from the ballpark speakers. Smoltz finished his illustrious career with 27 postseason starts. All but this one lasted at least 5⅔ innings.

Not so easy: Reliever Brad Clontz cleaned up Smoltz's mess by inducing a double play off the bat of Ramirez, who sent a one-hopper to second baseman Mark Lemke. McGriff and Klesko clubbed solo homers to trim the Braves' deficit, and the Indians unraveled in the eighth. Charles Nagy allowed a double to Marquis Grissom and an RBI single to Polonia, which cut the Tribe's lead to 5–4. Hargrove turned to his bullpen, but a walk, an error, and a single staked Atlanta to a 6–5 advantage. No team had ever erased a 3–0 series deficit in the postseason, and the Indians were teetering on the brink of unfavorable history.

The duel: Alomar's RBI double to right field tied the game and set the stage for a prize fight between two elite closers.

Wohlers recorded the final two outs in the bottom of the eighth.

Jose Mesa tiptoed around a single and a walk to escape unharmed in a 30-pitch top of the ninth.

Wohlers retired the Indians in order in the bottom of the ninth on nine pitches.

Mesa shut down the middle of the Braves' order in the top of the 10th.

Wohlers worked around a pair of walks in the bottom of the 10th.

Back and forth and back and forth while those in attendance inhaled and exhaled and chomped on their fingernails.

Mesa got Grissom to bounce into a double play to make for an easy top of the 11th and to outlast his counterpart. Mesa totaled 52 pitches in three scoreless innings, both season highs. Wohlers bowed out after 2⅔ scoreless frames, and the Indians jumped on Peña, his replacement. Baerga doubled to right-center and tagged in pinch-runner Alvaro Espinoza. Peña intentionally walked Belle, and Murray approached the plate. He was 0-for-5 with three strikeouts, but he attacked Peña's first offering, a fastball at the letters, and sent a liner to center field. Grissom's throw sailed up the third-base line and Espinoza slid into home and, at 12:42 AM, he brushed the plate with his right hand for the winning run.

On the Indians' radio broadcast, Herb Score shouted, "Swung on, line drive, center field! Base hit! Here comes Espinoza around third. The throw to home plate, not nearly in time! The Indians win the game! The Indians have won their first World Series game since 1948, and they do it in 11 innings. A base hit by Eddie Murray and scoring from second base, Alvaro Espinoza. The Indians win it in 11."

The Indians moved to 15–1 in extra-inning games in 1995. They notched their first World Series victory since October 11, 1948, also against a team named the Braves (Boston). It was their second walk-off win of the postseason, and it allowed the city, the fans, and the players to breathe. The Indians were back in the series.

Final: Indians 7, Braves 6

Game 4: The Premonition

The Indians liked their chances to tie the series at 2–2. Braves manager Bobby Cox refused to deviate from his original plan of deploying left-hander Steve Avery in Game 4, rather than turn to Maddux on short rest. While the Indians were thrilled to avoid Maddux for another day, in four starts since mid-September, Avery had posted a 1.00 ERA. In 27 innings during that stretch, he allowed only 11 hits and he tallied 33 strikeouts.

Tribe righty Ken Hill, making his second career postseason start, had limited Justice to one hit in 25 at-bats in their previous encounters—and that hit came in August 1990. Now, Hill had been careful with Justice at times, issuing him 12 walks. But Justice had failed to record a hit in 22 consecutive at-bats against Hill entering Game 4 of the 1995 World Series. Hill tossed seven scoreless frames in his Game 4 outing against the Mariners in the ALCS. Both he and Avery went 10 days between starts leading into their duel.

Rapid Robert: Bob Feller, the winningest pitcher in franchise history and the leader in innings, strikeouts, and games started, threw out the ceremonial first pitch. Wearing a white cotton sweater over a shirt and tie, glasses, and an Indians cap, he raised his arms over his head and completed a sidearm toss to Alomar, who caught the ball just off the edge of the plate. Feller made a pair of starts during the Indians' most recent World Series triumph in 1948.

An eye for an eye: The game proceeded into the sixth inning before either team scratched across a run. In the top of the inning, Klesko crushed a Hill offering into the right-field seats. Hill dropped to a knee and turned his head to watch the baseball soar into the night and then lowered his head in disappointment. The instant he made contact, Klesko flipped his bat and raised both arms. The Braves' lead would be short-lived, though, as Belle answered in the bottom of the frame with an opposite field liner that snuck over the fence. Avery had worked him away, but Belle powered a 1–2 pitch beyond reach. Avery also walked three batters and committed a balk that inning, but he limited the Indians to the one run.

Gut punch: Polonia's RBI double ended Hill's evening in the seventh, and with his kryptonite now watching idly from the dugout bench, Justice delivered a two-run single with two outs off Assenmacher, who smacked his glove once the baseball broke through the infield.

Cox summoned Wohlers to protect Atlanta's 5–1 advantage in the bottom of the ninth, even though he had thrown 48 pitches not even 24 hours earlier. Ramirez greeted Wohlers with a solo home run. Wohlers didn't even turn to watch the ball disappear beyond the outfield wall. He simply looked to his manager in the dugout and flashed a quick thumbs-up to indicate he felt fine. With a lefty starter on the mound, Hargrove replaced Thome and Paul Sorrento in the starting lineup with Espinoza and Herbert Perry. Sorrento pinch-hit for Perry in the ninth and followed Ramirez's homer with a double to left field. Cox could tell that Wohlers simply didn't have it, which was understandable given his workload the previous night.

So with Thome, Alomar, and Lofton scheduled to bat—two of the three being lefties—he called for left-handed reliever Pedro Borbon to attempt to seal the Braves' victory. Borbon had not pitched in 19 days, not since the eighth inning of Game 3 of the NLDS against the Rockies at Coors Field.

Borbon had a premonition a few days earlier that he would close out the decisive game of the World Series and be hailed a hero. He told his wife about the dream. Now, this did not follow his exact script. This was Game 4, and the Braves would still need a fourth win in the series. But Borbon struck out Thome on a pitch that Lopez snagged down and away, enough so that the typically mild-mannered Thome barked at home-plate umpire John Hirschbeck on his journey back to the dugout. Alomar struck out swinging for the second out and Lofton lined out to right field to end the game. Wohlers was the first player to spill out of Atlanta's dugout to congratulate his fellow reliever.

Final: Braves 5, Indians 2

Game 5: Back to Georgia

History was not on the Indians' side. Since the best-of-seven format was instituted on an annual basis in 1922, only five teams had erased a 3–1 deficit to win the World Series.

1985: The Royals topped the Cardinals in St. Louis in Game 5 and at home in Games 6 and 7.

1979: The Pirates outscored the Orioles—whose roster included Murray and Martínez—15–2 over the final three games, including the final two in Baltimore.

1968: On two days' rest, Mickey Lolich out-dueled Bob Gibson with his third complete-game victory of the series, as the Tigers stormed back to capture the title at Busch Stadium.

1958: The Yankees completed their comeback on the road against the Milwaukee Braves and their ace, Warren Spahn, who sputtered in the 10th inning of his Game 6 start.

1925: The Pirates defeated the Washington Senators at Griffith Stadium in the nation's capital in Game 5 and then won the final two contests at Forbes Field in Pittsburgh.

That's five occurrences in nearly 75 years, and only three times did the eventual winner finish the deal on the road. To make the task even more daunting, the Indians would have to conquer Maddux, who was pitching on full rest.

A game of adjustments: Hitting coach Charlie Manuel called for some tweaks to the Indians' approach in the batter's box against Maddux. He urged his hitters to stand closer to the plate so they could reach Maddux's pitches as they tailed toward the outside corner. Manuel thought this would force Maddux to pitch inside and try to jam the Tribe's hitters. He also encouraged his batters to aim to hit the ball the opposite way, even if it meant taking an inside-out swing. That way, Maddux might not be so inclined to set up shop on the outer half of the plate. Belle followed Manuel's advice in his first at-bat, as he lined a two-run homer to right field—to nearly the exact same spot he targeted the night before against Avery—in the first inning.

Too close for comfort: In the ensuing at-bat, Maddux tossed a pitch up and in to Murray, who took exception to the chin music. Murray took a few paces toward the mound and the two exchanged words before home-plate umpire Frank Pulli and catcher Charlie O'Brien impeded Murray's progress. The dugouts emptied. Murray kept pointing to his head. Hershiser approached Maddux and asked if he was intentionally throwing at Murray. Maddux, of course, contended that he was simply trying to jam the veteran. Hershiser reminded Maddux he could throw inside without targeting the space near a batter's head, especially considering Maddux possessed unparalleled accuracy. Three innings later, Murray lined a pitch back at Maddux, who made the catch while nearly dropping to all fours to avoid impact.

One thousand paper cuts: The Braves tied the game in the fifth, with some assistance from the Indians. Klesko singled, Lemke reached on Hershiser's throwing error and, after a sacrifice bunt, Hershiser intentionally walked Dwight Smith to load the bases for Grissom, who hit a chopper to the left of the mound. Hershiser failed to scoop it up as his momentum carried him past the third-base line and toward the Indians' dugout. By the time Thome arrived at the baseball, all of the runners had advanced safely. So the Braves had erased their deficit and still had the bases loaded for Polonia, who had homered in the previous inning. Hershiser's only hope was to induce a sharply struck ground ball that his defense could convert into an inning-ending double play. Right on cue, Polonia sent a screamer to Vizquel, who flipped the ball to Baerga, who threw to first to help Hershiser escape further harm.

The breakthrough: The Indians had placed two runners aboard with two outs in the sixth against Maddux when Thome stepped up to the plate. Maddux got ahead in the count 1–2 and Thome planned for an off-speed pitch. He figured Maddux would try to lure him into swinging aimlessly at a pitch that plunged out of the strike zone. Maddux tossed him a changeup, low and away…just not as low and not as far away as Maddux would have preferred. Thome socked the pitch up the middle for a go-ahead single. Ramirez followed with another RBI single and the Indians claimed a 4–2 lead. It marked only the third time all season that Maddux had surrendered more than three runs.

The shutdown: Hershiser retired the Braves in order in the seventh, and he returned to the hill for the eighth inning, confident it would be his last. Mike Mordecai opened the frame with a single. Grissom lined the second pitch of his at-bat right back at Hershiser, who snagged the baseball and tossed it to first for a momentous double play. Instead of a single up the middle and the tying runs on base, Hershiser had neutralized Atlanta's threat. He repeatedly yelled, "Take that!" as he marched around the mound. He had atoned for his earlier defensive miscues, and he struck out Polonia to cap his eight-inning masterpiece. When the Indians needed him most, Hershiser out-pitched Maddux.

The insurance policy: Thome crushed a solo homer to center, clearing the very end of the 19-foot-high wall, with two outs in the eighth. He tossed aside his bat with a "won't be needing this anymore" sort of nonchalance. That provided the Indians with a three-run cushion, which proved critical, because Klesko crushed a two-run homer to right off Mesa in the ninth to make it 5–4. Klesko, the ultimate rude houseguest, homered in each of the three games at Jacobs Field. It was guaranteed to be the Indians' final home game of the season, so it figured they would make the finish as dramatic as possible. Mesa struck out Lemke to secure the win—and the fourth one-run game in the series—prompting broadcaster Al Michaels to say, "Back to Georgia."

The Braves would not be holding any celebration on Cleveland's turf.

Final: Indians 5, Braves 4

Game 6: Justice is Served

Thome proclaimed after Game 5 that if the Indians won Game 6, they would finish the deal in Game 7. "I believe that," he said. "This next game is going to be the biggest game of, I think, everybody's career." Hershiser asserted that all of the pressure was on the Braves as the series shifted to Atlanta. Vizquel contended that the Braves' past World Series shortcomings would haunt them and leave them unable to shut the door for a third time in five years.

Chipper Jones delivered a different declaration during the war of words.

"We came up here [to Cleveland] and we played pretty dang well, made things tough on them," he said. "Now they have to go into a hostile environment and beat us twice in our own backyard."

He shrugged, and then proceeded, "Hats off to 'em if they do it. I don't think they will."

Those comments took a backseat to the main headline that drew attention in anticipation of Game 6. Justice stirred up a controversy by saying Braves fans were not as fully invested in supporting the team as they had been during past postseason runs. The *Atlanta Journal-Constitution* ran a headline reading JUSTICE TAKES A RIP AT BRAVES FANS, which only irked Justice further and had the hornet's nest buzzing. Justice challenged the fan base to prove him wrong. He said he expected to be showered with boos during Game 6 introductions. He was right. But he was also correct about another thing. If the Braves captured the Commissioner's Trophy, the quarrel would become nothing but a footnote.

"Oh God, he took a lot of heat for that," Wiley said.

Getting presidential: Jimmy Carter, the 39th president of the United States and a Georgia native and former governor of the state, tossed out the ceremonial first pitch, one impressive enough to earn some praise from Bob Costas on the broadcast. "You know," Costas said, "if the ump wants to give him the high strike, that's right in there, and with some hop on it—43 [mph], we're told, on the radar gun. Not bad." Once Mordecai squeezed the first pitch, Carter walked off the field, hopped over the railing to his front-row seat, and hugged Jane Fonda, who was sitting beside him.

Bobbing and weaving: Martínez channeled his inner Harry Houdini to escape harm in the early innings. He allowed a pair of singles in the first, but Lemke was caught stealing to interrupt Atlanta's bid for a first-inning lead. Martínez walked the first two batters in the second inning, but Vizquel made a dazzling stop and underhand glove flip to Baerga seem so casual—in an "Oh, don't mind me, just pushing defensive limits with the season on the line and a national audience tuning in" sort of manner—to initiate a 6-4-3 double play. Martínez allowed a double and a couple of walks in the fourth, but again, the Braves failed to score. Meanwhile, aside from two Belle walks, Glavine completely stifled the Indians through five innings.

Early on, Justice could tell that Glavine was destined for a brilliant outing.

"The first inning, when I saw [home-plate umpire Joe Brinkman] giving him pitches off the plate, I said, 'We've got this,'" Justice told Wiley a couple years later. "'Nobody will hit him.' He could command the ball so well. All we had to do is score one."

The strike zone became a significant talking point during and after the series.

"There were times," Wiley said, "you look at that last game, where Manny Ramirez would have had to step on the plate to hit the ball. I'm not taking anything away from them. They could take advantage, and we could have done the same thing. We just probably didn't make as many good pitches."

Said Thome, "One thing that did stand out was, at times, the strike zone. Not to make excuses, but the strike zones, on both sides, they were bigger at times. But it was a great series. They pitched extremely well."

Decisions, decisions: With two outs in the bottom of the fifth, Martínez walked Lemke and served up a single to Jones. Hargrove made a slow stroll to the mound to change pitchers. Martínez exited after 4⅔ innings, having allowed four hits and five walks. He threw 82 pitches. It was far from a masterpiece—well, maybe a Jackson Pollock, given all the chaos going on around him—but as he retreated to the dugout, the scoreboard still read 0–0. Hargrove summoned left-hander Jim Poole, who struck out the lefty McGriff on three pitches to end the Braves' threat.

Tony Peña notched the Indians' first hit, a bloop single to center to start the sixth. Hargrove had a decision to make. He could leave Poole in to attempt a sacrifice bunt to advance Peña into scoring position. Or he could pinch-hit for Poole, who had never recorded a plate appearance. Hargrove wanted Poole to pitch to lefties Justice and Klesko in the sixth, so he took the risk. Poole bunted an 0–2 pitch in foul territory for a pop-out. The move backfired. Lofton and Vizquel could not scratch across a hit off Glavine, and Peña's leadoff single went for naught.

The backfiring wasn't over, either. Justice launched Poole's third pitch of the sixth inning over the right-field fence. The Braves had the lead. Costas declared, "Dave Justice, all is forgiven in Atlanta." Hargrove's intentions were sensible, given the Braves' powerful trio of lefties, but the decision could not have unfolded in a less favorable manner.

The final act: Glavine departed after eight flawless innings, the Peña bloop being the Indians' only base knock. Remember when

Belliard committed a first-inning gaffe in Game 1 that ultimately contributed to Lofton scoring the first run of the series? He earned some revenge in the ninth inning of Game 6, as he completed a long, running backhand grab in foul territory to retire Lofton. That allowed Wohlers to exhale a bit, as Lofton reaching base would alter the entire complexion of the inning. Sorrento flied out and, for the third time in three games at Fulton-County Stadium, Baerga—dealing all week with ankle injuries that caused him additional pain when he batted from the left side—made the final out, as Grissom hauled in his fly ball to left-center field.

On the Indians' radio broadcast, Score said, "Fly ball, left field. Back goes Grissom, still going back. He's there. The game is over. The Atlanta Braves have won the World Series. The Atlanta Braves are the champions of all of baseball."

"That was unbelievable," Wiley said. "I think we had the team that could have won it. I'm not taking anything away from the Braves, but we just came up short. That last game, I will never forget."

Belle was left on deck, that season's most prolific, most imposing hitter resigned to standing a bat flip from home plate with the World Series hanging in the balance. Some Indians players remained in the dugout and forced themselves to watch the Braves create a dog pile on the infield. Some hustled back to the clubhouse to remove themselves from a scene they wanted no part in witnessing. Others sat on the dugout bench and just stared forward, into oblivion, slowly accepting the cruel fate of a baseball season that unfolds in rapid, nonstop fashion for more than six months before crashing head-first into a brick wall.

"It was a really quick ending to a great year," Sorrento said. "We didn't think we were going to lose. We never had that thought in our head. Hats off to the Braves. They played a great series. They beat us. It was a disappointing ending. I didn't think it was going to end that way.

Kenny KOs the K Zone

The only thing that stands out about the World Series is that we should have won the World Series. We didn't, and I just felt, to be honest, it was taken away from us. We had the highest on-base percentage. We had the most runs scored. We had the most walks. We had the fewest amount of strikeouts. Then all of a sudden, the World Series, that changed. Nothing changed throughout the baseball game. The bases, the strike zone, the diamond. Nothing changed. But for us to have a good eye at the plate and have someone take that away from us, it confused all of us. We knew what was a ball and what was a strike, because we did it all year. And then we came to the World Series and all of a sudden, somebody told us a ball off the plate this far [spreads his hands apart] is a strike. No, it's not a strike. And we knew that throughout the year, that eight inches off the plate is not a strike. Off the plate is a ball. And we had to deal with that. So we had to go out of our norm to try to make adjustments. We had a bad enough time making adjustments to the pitchers. We had to make adjustments to the umpires. That wasn't a cool thing to do.

So I separate it by saying it was taken away. We did not lose the World Series. I'm going to keep my head high because we did not lose the World Series. It was given to the Braves. Bottom line. That World Series was handed to them on a silver platter. And I will say that to anybody's face. It was handed to them.

—Kenny Lofton

"I had been there with Minnesota and won it, and then to be there and lose it, I remember it was really hard. We ran up against Smoltz, Glavine, and Maddux, which was no easy task."

Final: Braves 1, Indians 0

"It was funny," Wiley said. "When we went to the playoffs, I can't honestly think that we ever thought we would lose in the playoffs on the way to the World Series. I just think our guys knew we were good enough and we were going to do this and we got to the World Series and we faced a Hall of Fame pitching staff. They knew what the hell they were doing. We had a lot of tight games, 3–2, 1–0, and all of that.

"We won a lot of games and we were a great team. We could have won the World Series. But we never had that one guy, like a Pedro [Martínez] or a [Curt] Schilling or a Randy [Johnson]. We didn't have that one guy who was a beast who could just outstep you for nine innings. We had really professional guys who knew what they were doing, but we didn't have those kinds of guys. I think, when you're in the World Series, and you don't have a guy like that—you have to have some horses. To win the World Series, you have to have a [Justin] Verlander. You have to have a [Clayton] Kershaw. You have to have a horse. Or two."

The Indians, of course, had a chance to acquire Pedro Martínez after the 1997 season—for a package including Jaret Wright and Bartolo Colon—and Randy Johnson during the '98 season, but John Hart rebuffed trade offers for his top prospects.

The Braves, on the other hand, had several front-line workhorses in their rotation. Glavine and Wohlers combined to log the fifth one-hitter in World Series history. It marked the Indians' first 1–0 loss since May 20, 1992, against the Texas Rangers at Cleveland

Stadium before a whopping 6,687 people. The Indians dropped to 13–28 on that Wednesday night.

Their lineup:

CF Kenny Lofton

DH Alex Cole

2B Carlos Baerga

1B Paul Sorrento

RF Mark Whiten

C Sandy Alomar Jr.

LF Thomas Howard

3B Brook Jacoby

SS Tony Perezchica

Charles Nagy tossed a complete game, throwing 125 pitches in the loss.

They had come a long way in three and a half years. But they still fell short of their ultimate goal. And that stinging feeling would take some time to subside.

"We just thought this was our moment," Lofton said, "this was our time."

And so, there was no immediate appreciation for everything the Indians accomplished in 1995. When Grissom squeezed that final out, it was difficult for the Indians to feel anything but disappointment.

"I think that comes later," Hargrove said. "When you first lose, it's crushing. And there's not a whole lot of room for thoughts of, 'What a great year.' Even though it had been. It takes a while for that to settle in."

14

"Just Talking About It Gives You Chills"

THE PLANE DUG ITS WHEELS into the runway and a 100-minute flight from Atlanta to Cleveland—which, for a 100-win team that came up short in its bid for a championship, seemed more like 100 hours—reached its conclusion. The team received a police escort from the airport back to Jacobs Field, and as the bus sped down the highway, there they were.

Fans. Everywhere.

They lined the chain-linked fence at the airport, holding signs and waving flags and reaching through the small gaps in the fence to shake hands with the players. They pulled over in their cars on the side of I-71. They propped open their doors, stood up, and applauded the players as the bus whizzed past. They arrived in droves in downtown Cleveland, where they greeted the team at the ballpark, just a handful of hours after a crushing Game 6 defeat in the franchise's first World Series appearance in 41 years.

"It was a surreal moment," Sandy Alomar Jr. said. "You lose the World Series and people in Cleveland are starving for a winner. I don't even know what time it was. It was late. And the airport was packed with people. And then they had a parade, even though we were the losing team in the World Series. That meant the world. And I think that really showed to the players how much Cleveland cared and how much they wanted us to succeed."

October baseball was a new concept to the city. The franchise had essentially hibernated for four decades, save for the annual summer disappointment on the shores of Lake Erie, where mayflies outnumbered fans in the stadium seats. There was never any hope. There were never any expectations—well, so long as Joe Carter and Cory Snyder were not gracing the cover of *Sports Illustrated*. There were never any *legitimate* expectations.

The process of building toward the 1995 season was an intricate labyrinth, and the proper path to 100 wins and the start of a potential dynasty was filled with fortune, patience, and perfect timing. The Indians needed certain legislation to pass. They needed certain trades to pan out, certain prospects to blossom. They needed certain free agents to believe in their sales pitch and provide a young roster with some sorely needed guidance. They needed Albert Belle to channel his frustration toward opposing pitchers' fastballs and Jose Mesa to embrace the ninth inning. They needed fans to buy in to the idea that this was different, a new chapter to brighten an old, tired saga. But when it all came together, it produced perhaps the most memorable season in franchise history, even though it lacked the final cherry on top.

For once, fans had reason to believe, reason to invest their time and their energy. They had motivation to pass through the turnstiles, to purchase a Kenny Lofton jersey, to meet the team in the middle of the night after a heartbreaking loss just to offer one final show of support.

"The biggest part of that was you could see the city really coming to life," Jim Thome said. "Once the '95 season was over, I think people were like, 'Okay, this is a really good ball club.' Our fans believed it. We believed it. People in baseball started believing it. I tell guys, 'When you get an opportunity to go to the postseason, cherish it.' I have to be honest—for years, I thought we were always going, with the teams we had. If you are lucky to play a long time, you realize it's just not that easy. I don't want to say you take it for granted, but you want to make sure you don't."

The atmosphere on a plane ride often hinges on the on-field results that preceded it. A cross-country flight following a winless trip to the West Coast? A library full of mimes would be noisier. A trip back to Cleveland after a playoff series victory? The scent of champagne would surely follow the players onto the aircraft, as would loud music, laughter, and plenty of chatter.

Now consider a team that blitzed through the regular season, with 10 more wins than any other club. It made thrilling walk-off wins a regular occurrence. It made life miserable for opposing pitchers. It treated its long-deprived fan base to a magical journey that persisted until the final few days of October, a portion of the calendar the franchise had never traversed. And then the season sputtered against the Braves' stout pitching staff. Would they have accepted the terms to the 1995 season—100 wins, an unparalleled amount of fun, and a World Series appearance—when they reported to spring training in Winter Haven? Yeah, those conditions probably would have been difficult to reject. That would have been considered a prolific season, even without the rings that the Braves ultimately claimed.

But expectations evolve throughout a season, and the Indians had built up this idea—not a far-fetched one, either—that they could not be topped. So that made the eventual outcome even tougher to stomach. The Indians spent the entire year landing knockout punch after knockout punch; this was the first time all season that an opponent had returned a right hook. As Mike Hargrove noted, the Indians encountered very little adversity in 1995 until the World Series. They simply squashed everything standing in their way—until the end.

"After a loss, we didn't take it lightly," Carlos Baerga said. "We would think about it. We used to stay in the clubhouse for a long time. If we lost two games in a row, that hit us right away and we would say, 'Hey, we have to come back the next day.'"

Only after Game 6, there was no next day. And that's what made it so challenging, the attempt to separate the final feeling from the sentiment toward what had undoubtedly been an iconic season in franchise lore. In the immediate aftermath of a season-ending loss, a player's competitive spirit will not allow for fond thoughts of what was unquestionably a year to remember. There's a grieving period, and the first stage is disappointment, no matter the circumstances.

"We were disheartened," Thome said. "We wanted to win a World Series. I think what put it in perspective is how our fans showed up.

"It sure would've been nice for this city to accomplish that. That's the biggest thing, is knowing what it could have done to the city of Cleveland. I think about how proud they would have been of us doing it and the support they showed."

Two days after Game 6, the city hosted a rally in downtown Cleveland to celebrate the Indians' revival. Tens of thousands of fans lined the streets and filled in every nook and cranny in Public Square, where a giant stage was set up for players, coaches, and front office executives to address the crowd. Player banners adorned every light post in front of the Terminal Tower. Fans toted signs and donned Indians garb on that penultimate day of October. They screamed and chanted and shook cowbells.

A group of police officers on motorcycles first created a path down Superior Road, adjacent to Public Square, with a row of police on horseback behind them. Next came a line of cars, followed by a series of high school marching bands and cheerleaders. Band members had players' names and numbers inscribed on their instruments; one tuba displayed BELLE with the No. 8. A few decked-out trucks drove past. One revealed a banner that read: WAHOO, WHAT A SEASON! WAHOO, WHAT A FINISH!! WAHOO, WHAT A TEAM!!!

As the players made their way up to the stage, fans jockeyed for position to attain the best possible view. One person even scaled a cylinder post to stand atop the crosswalk sign. Others stood atop newspaper stands or jumped up and down, all to catch a glimpse of their heroes.

A group of aliens could have parked their UFO on Ontario Street, exited the spacecraft, and assumed the Indians had emerged victorious against the Braves in the World Series. Nothing about the scene on that chilly, overcast Monday indicated that Cleveland had come up short. Everyone in attendance was simply appreciative of what the Indians had achieved, especially given the lack of buzz around the franchise the previous 41 years. And that jumpstarted an unequaled rapport between the team and the fan base that would last through the end of the decade, a relationship captured by the retired No. 455 at the ballpark, in honor of the fans' record sellout streak.

"People just loved us," Omar Vizquel said. "No matter where you would go—autograph sessions, the clinic, anywhere—people were just in tune with the team. They felt like part of [the team]. And we felt like part of the community. That was the most awesome relationship that we could have."

Said Thome, "It was overwhelmingly positive, the feeling. I think at that point, we as players knew, 'Wow. Our fans are really behind us and we have something special here.'"

Paul Shuey lives in Raleigh, North Carolina. He keeps in touch with Thome and Travis Fryman. He goes fishing with Eric Plunk. In his area, the Durham Bulls, the minor league affiliate for the Tampa Bay Rays, receive a decent amount of attention. There is no major league team nearby. Yet locals often mention the '90s Indians to him, with the '95 team representing the first-born child who could do no wrong.

"It still carries a lot of weight, I'll put it that way," Shuey said. "Those teams were so special to everybody who was in Cleveland or who watched Cleveland baseball. Just talking about it gives you chills. It was special. I didn't know that the guys were as good as they were at the time. I knew they were good..."

His voice drifted off. Shuey was still finding his footing in the majors at that point, still attempting to overhaul an excessive leg kick and still technically a rookie, despite breaking into the big leagues in 1994. He was an alternate for the postseason roster in '95, so he remained on a throwing regimen in October in case a pitcher suffered an injury and needed to be replaced. For a 25-year-old without much big-league experience, it was unforgettable, even watching from a bit of a distance. Shuey has fond memories of the police escorts chaperoning the Indians through each city in the playoffs.

"Just being part of that," Shuey said, "it was just so cool. Looking back on it now, I wish I had been further along to where I had the lower leg kick and I could hit my spots and was more of a professional pitcher. But it was wild and crazy at that point in time. It was epic."

The downtown festivities helped to free the Indians from the dissatisfaction they felt two nights earlier as the Braves soaked the home clubhouse at Fulton-County Stadium with enough alcoholic beverages to fill the Cuyahoga River. The event reassured the Indians of what they already knew—this was just the beginning.

Sure, a championship would have capped an absolutely flawless season and crowned the 1995 Indians as one of the greatest teams in league history. But the Indians knew they would be back. They would win one. At least one. The front office had not torn the roster to the studs and gradually assembled a robust farm system just for one crack at the postseason. The 1995 season was intended to serve as a springboard toward a lengthy run of success. And now, there would be no surprises, no more firsts to get out of the way. Every player on the roster knew what to expect, knew what challenges October baseball could present, and knew how to navigate a season from start to finish.

The Indians repeated as AL Central champions in 1996 and '97 and '98 and '99 and '01. They returned to the World Series in '97 but suffered a nightmarish late-inning collapse—it felt like it unfolded in slow motion—in Game 7 in south Florida. Alomar has never re-watched that game, despite it occasionally surfacing on ESPN Classic or on YouTube, and despite friends texting him to tell him he's on TV, not realizing the ultimate fate of the episode.

Hargrove once asked Mark Wiley if he has ever re-watched the '90s Indians' two World Series appearances. He has seen highlights or footage from various games in both series, but never the final installments. He has never re-watched Game 6 of the 1995 World Series or Game 7 of the 1997 World Series. To make matters worse, Wiley lived in the Miami area in '97.

"I took some heat after that game from people in my neighborhood," Wiley said.

The '95 season certainly was not the Indians' only chance to attain glory. The '96 Indians won 99 games but fizzled in the ALDS against the Orioles. John Hart traded Baerga and Eddie Murray during that season, and the roster face lift continued into

1997 as Belle bitterly departed via free agency and the Indians swapped out Lofton and Alan Embree for Marquis Grissom and David Justice. The '97 team never found its footing until late August, when players celebrated Thome's 27th birthday by hiking up their pant legs to reveal high socks. The unifying measure sparked the 86-win club to a surprising run to the World Series, though that resulted in another painful reminder of the franchise's misfortunes during its lengthy title drought. Orel Hershiser claimed some responsibility, saying if he would have pitched better in October in either '95 or '97, the Indians might have enjoyed a winter as league champions.

The '98 team won 89 games, but ran into a juggernaut Yankees squad that had racked up 114 victories during the regular season. The Indians actually led the ALCS 2–1 through three games— New York's only two defeats during its postseason march to its first of three consecutive championships. The '99 team won 97 games and became the first club to eclipse the 1,000-run mark in nearly a half-century, but inconsistent pitching caught up with the Indians in the ALDS. The Red Sox stormed back from a 2–0 deficit to knock out Cleveland in the first round, scoring 44 runs in the final three tilts of the five-game series, and ultimately costing Hargrove his job. The 2000 team cycled through 32 different pitchers en route to 90 wins, one short of the number necessary for a playoff berth. It snapped Cleveland's division title streak at five. The '01 team rebounded, winning 91 games and the AL Central, but the club tripped up in the ALDS against the 116-win Mariners, who recovered after falling behind 2–1 in the series.

"The fans supported us in '96, '97, '98, '99, and on," Alomar said. "I think the players wanted to give the fans their gift. We pushed hard in '96. It wasn't there. But '97, we were back in the World Series, and unfortunately we lost in Game 7. That could have gone either way. But we really did appreciate what the fans did during those times. It was fantastic. The support was incredible."

Players from the '95 team had their legacies etched in stone—quite literally. Thome's statue stands tall outside the center-field gate at Progressive Field, his bat pointed toward E. 9th Street. Hargrove, Alomar, Belle, Lofton, Thome, Vizquel, Carlos Baerga, and Charles Nagy are all Indians Hall of Fame inductees, with plaques commemorating the honor in Heritage Park, beyond the center field wall at the ballpark.

"Years later, I was coaching for other teams," Wiley said, "and I would talk to players all over the game that were with the Indians [back then] and we're going, 'Were those great years or what?' And they were still playing! That's when you know you had a good team. You look at those teams and look at how long those players played. They all played over 10 years. It's crazy.

"We had ridiculous players."

Vizquel stuck with the Indians the longest, through the 2004 campaign, his 11th season in Cleveland. After that, he relocated to San Francisco, where he spent four seasons with the Giants and captured the final two Gold Glove Awards of his career (his 10th and 11th overall). He played for four more years, 2009-12, with the Rangers, White Sox, and Blue Jays, all AL teams. So each season, he made at least one trip back to Cleveland. He fondly remembers the Indians playing a two-minute video montage to welcome him back on each occasion, the local newspaper printing a report about his return and his illustrious Cleveland career, and the fans rewarding him with a standing ovation every time he stepped into the batter's box while donning the jersey of the opposing team.

"I kept saying, 'Man, I've been out of Cleveland already for seven years,'" Vizquel said, "'and people are still writing and doing all of this beautiful stuff for me. These people are really special.' Obviously, I made some kind of impact with the fans in order for them to still be able to do all of this stuff. Every time I played in Cleveland, it was something different. It was really, really nice.

"Cleveland opened tons of doors for me, possibilities to try to do new stuff. It was awesome. The connection that we had with the fans was really amazing. Everywhere you would go, they had to talk about the team and [tell] stories. Even the policemen stopped by my house to ask for autographs. We had a really close community there. It was amazing just to be in that town. I really cried the day that they said they were not going to sign me. It was a long time, 11 years, that I played in Cleveland. I wanted to retire with the Indians, but in professional [sports] nowadays, it's pretty hard, all the business you go through, all the contracts and guys coming up and all that stuff. It was a really melancholy moment for me, but I understood the business."

The Indians inducted Vizquel into their Hall of Fame in 2014. As Vizquel trotted in from the bullpen to deliver his induction speech at a podium on the infield, Baerga flipped him a baseball. Vizquel leaped in the air and made a bare-handed snag, a familiar sight for the sellout crowd. Baerga and Vizquel perfected that relay from 1994 to '96. After his speech, Vizquel hopped in his patented yellow Porsche convertible and took a lap around the field.

The day before the ceremony, Vizquel, then the Tigers' first base coach, made the drive from Detroit to Cleveland along the Ohio Turnpike. He stopped at an exit near Sandusky to grab something to drink. He pulled up to the turnpike toll booth and the woman working in the ticket window recognized him and begged

Vizquel to get out of his car to take a picture with her. Vizquel couldn't believe it.

But people remember. They remember how the 1995 team officially placed the four-decade stretch of misery in the rearview mirror. They remember how that launched a seven-year run of entertaining baseball in downtown Cleveland. They remember how the '95 team made it chic, made it fun, and made it widely acceptable to fall in love with baseball in Cleveland again.

"You don't realize what kind of team and what kind of teammates you have until you see it now from where we are," Vizquel said. "You look back and say, 'Wow, those guys were amazing. We had one of the greatest teams ever.'"

A World Series triumph against the Braves certainly would have made this a less complex debate. The 1995 Indians would have been regarded as one of the best teams of all-time, a club that simply steamrolled its competition for six months, with an unrivaled lineup that not even a Hall of Fame–heavy starting rotation could contain and with an underrated pitching staff full of savvy veterans. After all, they established a new MLB record by finishing the season with a 30-game lead in the division, eclipsing the previous record of 27½ games set by the 1902 Pittsburgh Pirates. (Credit to Fred Clarke's scrappy bunch, which included Hall of Famer Honus Wagner and three 20-game winners with ERAs around the 2.00 mark.)

"When I see other teams get to a certain point," Wiley said, "I go, 'That team is getting close to what we were. Teams don't think they can beat them.' You get that little bit of negative thinking into a major league team's head, they're done. The self-fulfilling prophecy happens all the time."

But the World Series result, to some, places the '95 Indians into a sort of awkward gray area. For all but the final week of the season, the Indians seemed like an unconquerable beast destined to end the franchise's championship drought. But the Braves tamed the beast, so the legacy is a bit complicated.

"I guess it's just what boat you fall in," Paul Sorrento said. "If you have to win it to be a great team, we didn't, so a lot of people will say that we weren't that great, because we didn't win it. But I think just the way we went through that season—we were head and shoulders above everybody else. It just played out in the long run. It showed that. But we didn't win it, so I don't know. I guess we can't be called a great team. It's just like all of those Buffalo Bills teams. You look back now at that feat and it's unbelievable that they got to the Super Bowl four years in a row, even to lose it. But do you call them great teams? I don't know."

The '95 Indians are undoubtedly one of the top teams *not* to win a title. That year remains the golden standard in Cleveland, at least for those not old enough to remember Lou Boudreau's hitting (and managing) prowess or Bob Lemon's rubber arm or Bill Wambsganss' unassisted triple play. Anyone associated with the '95 team is considered royalty, even if Alvaro Espinoza has never been stopped at a toll booth to pose for a stranger's photo.

"It's my favorite season," said Wiley, who has spent a half-century in the game. "No doubt. By far. In spring training [in 2019], I saw Sandy. He was with Cleveland and we were playing them and I was over there and I was in the bullpen talking to him. The first thing we just started talking about was that year, and those other years. But '95, it was ridiculous. It's like it's etched in our minds, exactly what happened. I can remember, I coached for 17 years in the big leagues.

It's hard for me to figure out who were on what teams. But I know every player that was on that '95 team."

In the bowels of Progressive Field resides a nondescript room, mostly empty aside from a barren counter and a collage of old Indians-related newspaper printouts tacked to a bulletin board on the wall. That room branches off into three others: one for storage, one for the team barber to chop players' hair, and one that serves as a photographer workspace, with equipment and loose notes scattered throughout the untidy area. At the back of that workroom is a dark, unmarked closet, and taped to the inside of the open door is a black-and-white photo of Babe Ruth, leaning on Bob Feller's bat as he addressed the Yankee Stadium crowd in 1948 for the final time. Two months after the photo was snapped, Ruth succumbed to cancer.

The lights in the closet don't function. The bulbs from the other rooms offer just enough illumination to highlight a bat rack, some organizers, and a couple of shelves that span the height of the far wall. The cramped space—cluttered, uninspiring and, unfortunately, mostly neglected—is actually a hidden vault of Indians memorabilia, a stash of historic possessions from one of the American League's charter franchises. Some items are prized, others mostly pointless. Some are obvious, others obscure. There are 70 boxes filled with signed balls and jerseys, old programs, ticket stubs, pennants, magazine covers, and newspaper clippings. It's an impressive collection of lasting images that highlight 120 years of Cleveland Indians history.

There is a base from the 2016 World Series, a selection of baseballs from the latter stages of the 2017 team's record 22-game winning streak, an invitation to a buffet luncheon at Municipal Stadium to honor Hall of Fame manager Connie Mack, a 1980 *Baseball Digest* cover featuring super rookie Joe Charboneau, and a Bob Feller candy bar wrapper. For five cents, one could purchase a 2.5-ounce sugary snack, "Made Fresh Every Hour For A Good Feller." There is a Western Union telegram, postmarked on January 25, 1962, with a message for Feller in block print:

MY MOST SINCERE CONGRATULATIONS
I AM HONORED TO GO INTO THE HALL OF FAME
WITH YOU

There is a $2 lower box ticket for the Indians' 1948 Opening Day tilt against the St. Louis Browns at Municipal Stadium and a canvas-sized ticket from Game 3 of the 1948 World Series, for which an upper reserve seat cost $6.25. There is a $6 upper reserve ticket for the 1963 All-Star Game, a two-hour, 20-minute afternoon affair played on a Tuesday in July on the lakefront. There is a special game ticket from 1973 in which the attendee was considered a guest of team owner Nick Mileti. There is a green ticket from a May 15, 1981, clash between the Indians and Blue Jays, ordinarily an unremarkable occasion if not for Len Barker recording Cleveland's first perfect game in 73 years. A lower box seat cost $7 that night.

A stack of old lineup cards rests atop a pile of caricatures of Shoeless Joe Jackson, Stan Coveleski, Joe Sewell, Ken Keltner, Steve O'Neill, Hal Trosky, and others who played for the Indians in the early part of the 20th century. A framed team photo of the 1907 club—a Nap Lajoie–led, 85-win team—rests against a wall. There is a June 1976 copy of *Baseball Digest*, with Rick Manning on the cover, beneath the headline: EXCLUSIVE! THESE ARE MAJORS' MOST VALUABLE CENTER FIELDERS. There are old game programs, including one from 1993 that features the title, HARD WORKIN' PAUL SORRENTO. Greg Swindell, a former first-round draft pick who pitched for the Indians from 1986 to '91 and again in 1996, graces the cover of a 1989 program that simply collects dust.

The bat rack stores more than 40 pieces of lumber, including a Frank Robinson model from 1976, a Jason Kipnis model from May 2015 when he produced 51 hits, and the stick Carlos Santana used to power the Indians to victory in the 19th inning in Toronto on July 1, 2016, the team's then-franchise record 14th consecutive win.

The team salvaged Jay Bruce's navy uniform top from the night the 2017 team pushed its winning streak to 22 games. His teammates' tugging at the jersey during the postgame celebration damaged some of the piping and caused a tear in the neck of the uniform. There is a José Ramírez Father's Day jersey, with bright blue letters and numbers, from the day the All-Star infielder slugged a home run from both sides of the plate. There is a baseball with a yellow blemish, a bruise supplied by the right field foul pole, which absorbed Francisco Lindor's momentous grand slam in Game 2 of the 2017 AL Division Series. There is a box of baseballs signed by alumni who have passed through the ballpark in recent years, such as Fryman, Grissom, Richie Sexson, Paul Assenmacher, and Mike Jackson.

And, of course, there is a trove of 1995 memorabilia. There is a bright orange Wheaties box, stored in the Indians' archives room at Progressive Field, with a price sticker of $2.66. On the front cover, Jose Mesa grips a baseball with his thumb, index finger, and middle finger and Lofton stares down a pitcher while he prepares to swing his bat. The box was released in October 1995, complete with an AL CHAMPIONS banner and a pair of World Series logos.

There is a baseball and a program saved from the World Series and the red, white, and blue bunting that was on display at the Kingdome in Seattle during the AL Championship Series. There are ALDS tickets and a set of three ALCS tickets. There is a ticket stub from the game on May 22 against the Brewers and a ticket stub from the game on September 7 against the Mariners (a 4–1 win that pushed the Indians to the brink of securing their first postseason berth in 41 years). There is a ticket from Game 3 of the World Series, the Indians' first Fall Classic victory since 1948, and a ticket to Game 1 of the ALDS, a night the ticket user could not have anticipated lasting past 2:00 AM. There is a scorecard from an April game, a World Series jersey patch and bumper sticker, a season yearbook, and a Sorrento game-worn cap. When sifting through the memories of 120 years of Indians baseball, it is impossible not to stumble upon some memento from 1995.

Perhaps no team in Indians history captured Cleveland's imagination like the 1995 team did. Fans experienced a summer-long high that never wore off until the end of October. And even when the team ultimately fell short, they gathered at Public Square to demonstrate their appreciation for such an unthinkably exhilarating ride.

"Credit the fans," Thome said, "because they are the ones who were the driving force behind our success of the '90s. Really, I feel blessed that I was able to come to the big league level during that time, to be a part of those great, great '90s teams."

Lofton spent 17 seasons in the major leagues. He appeared in 2,103 games and suited up for 11 different big-league franchises. He even returned to Cleveland for his swan song in 2007, when he was 40 years old. When asked which season is his favorite, he does not hesitate.

"Ninety-five. It stands out the most," he said, "because of what we accomplished as a team. The '94 season was getting us in that direction and then '95 just took it over the top. We had the strike season in '94 and then we had the shortened season because of the strike. But for us to accomplish what we accomplished in that amount of games, it was extraordinary. We were in there as a group. We saw it. We did it. So we knew exactly what we did that year.

"Once the years go by and you start to compare, they say, 'That '95 Cleveland team was something else.' That's what really makes it sink in."

Lofton's perspective is particularly compelling, because he was no stranger to the October stage. He returned to the postseason with the Indians in '96, '98, '99, '01, and '07. In 1997, following his shocking trade to Atlanta, the Braves were upset by the Marlins in the NLCS. In 2002, he played for the Giants, who lost Game 7 of the World Series. In 2003, he played for the Cubs, who came one post-Bartman meltdown from advancing to face the Yankees in the Fall Classic. In 2004, he reached the ALCS with the Yankees, the first team to ever squander a 3–0 advantage in a best-of-seven series. In 2006, his Dodgers bowed out in the NLDS against the Mets.

Lofton shared a clubhouse in Atlanta with perhaps the greatest starting rotation ever assembled. He shared an outfield with Barry Bonds, who produced an otherworldly 1.381 OPS in 2002. Lofton played on 100-win teams and several World Series favorites.

But the one with an endless supply of magic, the one that gifted a tortured fan base a summer full of memories, the one that will forever stand out in his mind as the best team for which he ever played…was it the 1995 Indians?

"The best ever," Lofton said. "Yes."

Acknowledgments

THANK YOU to Jim Folk, Bob DiBiasio, Bart Swain, and Jeremy Feador of the Cleveland Indians for their assistance with various interviews or research. Thank you to the former players, coaches, and front office executives who agreed to spend some time reminiscing about such a special season.

Sources

Newspapers
The Atlanta Journal Constitution
Los Angeles Times
The New York Times
The Plain Dealer

Video
Fox Sports Ohio
Wahoo! What a Finish

Websites
The Athletic
The Associated Press
Baseball-Reference.com
Cleveland.com
FanGraphs
MLB.com